W9-DFV-229

*Yesterday's Columbus*

GEORGE E. CONDON

# Yesterday's

# COLUMBUS

A Pictorial History of Ohio's Capital

*Seemann's Historic Cities Series No. 31*

E. A. Seemann Publishing, Inc.
*Miami, Florida*

THE ILLUSTRATIONS in this book came from many sources, all indicated in abbreviated form at the end of each caption, and author and publisher wish to express their gratitude for the cooperation of so many sources, both public and private. A guide to the abbreviations follows:

| | |
|---|---|
| Bell | Ohio Bell Telephone Company, Columbus |
| Burke | Thomas Aquinas Burke Collection, Columbus |
| C&SOE | Central & Southern Ohio Electric Company, Columbus |
| C&C-J | *Columbus Citizen-Journal* |
| CD | *Columbus Dispatch* |
| CGS | Columbia Gas System, Columbus |
| CPD | *Cleveland Plain-Dealer* |
| CPL | Columbus Public Library |
| CU | Capital University, Columbus |
| Lazarus | Lazarus Collection, Ohio Historical Society, Columbus |
| OHS | Ohio Historical Society |
| OSU | Ohio State University Archives, Columbus |
| Weisheimer | Carl H. Weisheimer Collection, Columbus |

The photograph at the top of page **88** is reprinted from *The First Hundred Years: A Family Album of the Ohio State University, 1870-1970,* compiled and edited by the Department of Photography and Cinema at the University, and published in observance of the Centennial of the founding of the institution. Copyright © 1970 by the Ohio State University Press. All rights reserved.

**LIBRARY OF CONGRESS CATALOGING IN PUBLICATION DATA**

Condon, George E
   Yesterday's Columbus.

   (Seemann's historic cities series; No. 31)
   Includes index
   1. Columbus, Ohio—History—Pictorial works.
 2. Columbus, Ohio—Description—Views. I. Title.
F499.C7143C66   977.1'57'00222     77-9879
ISBN 0-912458-94-1

MW 6β JH EG PG HH

# Contents:

c . 1

COLUMBUS ACADEMY, a log structure built in 1820, was one of the earliest schools in the state capital. (OHS)

# *Acknowledgements*

LIKE MOST BOOKS, this one about the City of Columbus is the end product of many minds and many hands. It is the work, truly, of a group effort. Some persons and some institutions helped more than others, of course, but everyone was earnest and sincere in the manner of cooperation. In the face of that splendid spirit, the creation of *Yesterday's Columbus* was as much pleasure as it was work.

It is not possible, because of space limitations, to describe fully the extent of the assistance given by each individual named, but the reader is safe in assuming in each instance that it was considerable.

Among those, then, to whom I am grateful, are Edward R. Lentz, chief, audiovisual archives, Ohio Historical Society; William V. Merriman, director of communication services, Ohio State University; Thomas Aquinas Burke, collector of Columbus and Franklin County history and an authority on all things having to do with the Central Ohio area; Mayor Tom Moody, whose affection for the city he leads is genuine; Jack Huddle, director, Department of Development, City of Columbus; Dennis Brandon, division of planning, Department of Development, City of Columbus; Carl H. Weisheimer, Columbus authority and collector of historical items; Miss Ruth Jones, archivist, Ohio State University; James D. Hartshorne, former deputy director of the Ohio Turnpike Commission; Ben Hayes, columnist, *Columbus Citizen-Journal*; Richard Campbell, editor, *Columbus Citizen-Journal*; Preston Wolfe, retired publisher, *The Columbus Dispatch*; Mel Tharp, vice-president of *The Columbus Dispatch*; James Hunter, librarian, *The Columbus Dispatch;* Carl deBloom, executive editor, *The Columbus Dispatch*; Samuel Roshon, head of the Columbus and Ohio history division, Columbus Public Library; Gene D'Angelo, general manager, WBNS-TV; Robert Zimmerman, vice-president, Columbus Chamber of Commerce; Frank Avren, public relations consultant; Mrs. Harriet Bracken, vice-president, Huntington National Bank; Kline Roberts, president, Columbus Chamber of Commerce; Robert Boyd, Columbus & Southern Ohio Electric Company; Edward Clark, chief photographer, Ohio Fuel Gas Division, Columbia Gas Company; Don Hollenback, publisher, *The Booster*; Weldon Kefauver, director, Ohio State University Press; and Fred Pfening, Jr.

Columbus is fortunate in commanding the love and loyalty of men and women like these.

*George E. Condon*

[ 7 ]

ITINERANT ARTISTS instead of wandering photographers roamed the countryside in the early years of the nineteenth century capturing, with their pens dipped in idealistic ink, such scenes as this estate called Eden Loin, the residence of one J. B. Powell of Truro Township in Franklin County. (CC-J)

# The Beginning Years: 1812 to 1825

MOST CITIES are born out of natural circumstances. They form spontaneously at cross-roads, at the mouths of rivers, close to important resources. They begin as tiny, shapeless amoeba, multiplying of themselves but also engulfing passersby and attracting adventurers, gradually growing in size and taking shape and form in what seems to be haphazard progression until one day they have blossomed out as distinct entities.

That is the way with most cities. But there are a few that fall into a different category. They are the ones that are deliberately brought into being to answer a purpose and to fill a need; that are created with their function and a sense of their form clearly in mind before the first tree has been felled or the first roof has been raised.

Columbus, Ohio, was such a place. It is one of the rare American cities that was foreseen, discussed, and studied before it existed and that then was fitted to a chosen site in conformity with a master plan. It was, in short, created to serve an important role as the capital of a yearling state, the very first state, indeed, to be taken out of the imperial sweep of the magnificent Northwest Territory.

Ohio had been able to operate out of provisional headquarters in Zanesville and Chillicothe after being admitted to the Union in 1803, but it was apparent by 1810 that the time had come to choose a permanent site of government. A five-man committee appointed by the legislature that year to find a satisfactory site knew what prerequisites were demanded.

The ideal location, according to the legislature's consensus, would have to be in the geographical center of the wilderness state. It would have to be a livable place, situated above the flood plain, accessible from all directions, close to the main routes of travel, promising in its resources, and as free of political entanglements as possible.

The choice of site, make no mistake, was a touchy political problem. There were a number of communities in the central part of Ohio that had declared themselves in contention for the honor; among these were Zanesville, Delaware, Lancaster, Franklinton,

Worthington, Circleville, Newark, and Westerville. Influential and eloquent spokesmen lobbied aggressively in their behalf.

After less than two years of study and one hastily buried decision (in favor of a pleasant piece of real estate that one day would sprout into the town of Dublin), the legislative committee in 1812 adroitly skirted the bids of existing communities and recommended acceptance of a proposition put forward by a group of four developers in Franklinton which called for the establishment of the new capital in virgin territory directly across from Franklinton, on the high east bank of the Scioto River.

The syndicate of developers consisted of Lyne Starling, James Johnston, Alexander McLaughlin, and John Kerr. The four men were residents of Franklinton, but when it became clear that their own town would not be tapped for state capital honors, they launched their campaign for the site across the Scioto, officially described as Township 5, Range 22, of the Refugee Lands. That name derived from the fact that the lands had been set aside by Congress after the Revolutionary War in behalf of people from Canada and Nova Scotia who had sympathized with the Revolutionary cause during the War of Independence and who, presumably, would become refugees after the war.

The Starling-Johnston-McLaughlin-Kerr syndicate promised that if the State of Ohio agreed to establish its permanent capital on the site, they would

(a) lay out the town,

(b) donate a ten-acre public square,

(c) donate a ten-acre plot of land for a penitentiary,

(d) construct a state house, state offices, a penitentiary, and such other buildings as the legislature would direct.

The legislature accepted the proposal on February 14, 1812, and, giving the developers more than five years to make good on their commitments, set the first session of the legislature in the new capital to begin on the first Monday of December 1817.

The contribution of a state legislator named Joseph Foos at that time cannot be overlooked. It was he, a representative from Franklin County, who suggested that the capital-to-be bear the name of Columbus.

The suggestion received a remarkable response. Even the most amiable and congenial of relatives will wrangle over the name of a new-born child, but there was instant, apparently unanimous approval of Columbus as a capital name. Amerigo Vespucci had snatched continental honors somehow, but there was never any doubt that Americans kept the explorer from Genoa close to their hearts. Columbia was the gem of the ocean; Columbus was an emerald that glittered in the heartland setting of Ohio. The name was a natural.

In that beginning day, all that stood on the east bank of the beautiful Scioto was a tall, heavy forest. Few areas in the country could match the fertility that awaited the white man in Central Ohio. The first explorers on the scene knew that it was a special kind of country. Glacial drift that had been spread evenly across the plain, only a short distance from the edge of the Appalachian plateau, had given rise to a thick stand of majestic trees, a forest of beeches, maples, elms, oaks, and hickory trees that awed even the grizzled pioneers who had seen the tall trees of the eastern wilderness.

The heavy tree cover was relieved only by occasional glades and by the open banks of

BROAD AND HIGH STREETS, the center of Columbus in the early years, as sketched by Henry Howe, the Ohio historian. To the left, along High Street, are, in order, the United States Court House, the State Office Building, and (with steeple) the first State House. To the right are the first Neil House and the American Hotel. (CC-J)

the sparkling rivers, the Scioto and what some of the earliest arrivals chose to call Whetstone Creek. Later, the original Indian name was restored, and it came again to be known as the Olentangy River. These two important waterways came together only a short distance away from the modest plot chosen to be the future seat of government.

Just across the Scioto, on the west bank, was the village of Franklinton, but its location was thought to promise future trouble because it was in a lowland area, more susceptible to flooding.

Some ten miles to the north of the capital site was the settlement called Worthington. It had been colonized by a company of about forty families from Connecticut and Massachusetts, the Scioto Company by name, under the leadership of Col. James Kilbourne. After preliminary exploration in 1803, the site had been purchased and settled beginning in May 1804.

Another pocket of pioneer settlers was to be found in the village of North Liberty, on Darby Creek, which had been laid out by Lucas Sullivant after the settlement of Franklinton. Otherwise, the lush countryside of Central Ohio was almost completely dominated by the forest. The scattering of tiny settlements, especially that of Franklinton, with its collection of rude huts, log cabins, and stores, however, did much to relieve the oppressive weight of total wilderness. The settlements also offered necessary services to the designers and builders of the new capital as it slowly came into being.

The legislative committee that decided the question of where to place the headquarters of the state government, by the way, could not claim credit as the first human beings to single out the site as something special. The ancient Mound Builders clearly had seen the advantages of the area in prehistoric times. Evidence of their ancient habitation was everywhere. The most prominent of the mounds that they left behind was one that stood in the early days where South High Street and Mound Street intersected. Civilization leveled the mound. There were no environmentalists or archaeologists on the scene in pioneer days.

At a much later date, several tribes of American Indians found the site to their liking. The most important of these groups were the Wyandots, but there also were encampments of Mingoes, Delawares, and Shawnees. The largest was a Wyandot settlement that was still inhabited when the vanguard of white explorers and settlers first moved into the region. It was on the bottom near the confluence of the Olentangy and the Scioto rivers, close to Spring Street and the later site of the Ohio Penitentiary.

There were no delays in getting the new capital underway. By springtime 1812, the layout of the town had been completed by Joel Wright of Warren County, hired by the state to make the basic design, and by Joseph Vance of Franklin County, his assistant.

It was a conservative design that showed a strong New England influence. The Wright-Vance team was generous and wise in the dimensions it allotted to the main thoroughfares, no doubt foreseeing the ceremonial as well as traffic needs of a future state capital. All streets, in their plan, were to cross at right angles. High Street would be 100 feet wide. Broad Street would be 120 feet across. All other main thoroughfares would be 82½ feet wide, and alleys 33 feet. In-lots would be 62½ feet in frontage width and 187½ feet deep. Out-lots on the east would contain about three acres each. A later addition to the plan called for out-lots also on the northern side of the town, and these would be over two acres each.

The first sale of lots began on June 18, 1812, the same day that the United States declared war against Great Britain, and continued for three days. Almost all of the lots sold were on High and Broad streets, and the prices ranged from $200 to $1,000 per lot.

In fulfillment of the syndicate's pledge, a penitentiary was built in 1813, and a 1½-acre graveyard, required by the agreement with the state, was opened for business.

The chips really flew as the axemen and builders went to work in earnest in the following year, 1814. The first church, a cabin on Spring Street, was built that year by the Presbyterians; the first school was constructed; the first newspaper made its appearance, *The Western Intelligencer*, transferred by its owner from Worthington and considered the forerunner of the *Ohio State Journal* and its successor, the *Citizen-Journal.* Most notable of all, the first State House was erected in the middle of the ten-acre public square.

The newborn town was officially incorporated as the Borough of Columbus on February 10, 1816. Among those elected to the first council at that time were Henry Brown, Michael Patton, Jarvis Pike, Robert and Jeremiah Armstrong, John Kerr, John Cutler, Caleb Houston, and Robert McCoy. The population, according to the first census taken in 1815, was 700 persons.

The new capital developed slowly, sometimes painfully so. It was not until 1816 that the last tree stumps were removed from High Street. The beginning years in the wilderness town with its crude huts and muddy, rutted roads tested the staying power and the endurance of all the pioneer residents. Far more threatening, however, were the epidemics that beset the settlement through the early decades. Cholera and influenza especially laid

THE FRANKLIN COUNTY COURT HOUSE at the southeast corner of High and Mound streets in the early part of the nineteenth century, in the city's formative period, was a grand structure that held its own for a long time. (CC-J)

siege periodically to the struggling town, and kept it under attack from autumn of 1823 to springtime of 1826. The diseases took such terrible toll that one eyewitness, Mrs. Betsy Green Deshler, wrote in October 1823, that there were "scarcely enough well people to bury the dead." She had described Columbus a few months earlier as "nothing but a scene of trouble, sickness and death."

In addition to the mysterious waves of illness that periodically swept the settlement, serious economic trouble darkened the Columbus scene in the 1820s. Two members of the original land syndicate, Alexander McLaughlin and James Johnston, had failed in business in the same year, 1820. The collapse of their fortunes was felt by the entire community. Their attempts to sell off large pieces of real estate at distress prices to stem the tide carrying them to disaster had an effect of worsening the situation generally. Other owners of real estate found themselves caught in the economic vortex and panicked by trying to unload their holdings at any price.

Eventually the sheriff and the U. S. marshall found themselves with a lot of land on their hands which was offered for bargain prices at public sale, but there weren't many takers. Lots that had been valued at $200 and $300 a few years before were unloaded for $10 and $20 bids.

McLaughlin and Johnston eventually lost their holdings and their wealth. John Kerr, another member of the original syndicate, died in 1823, and his estate was dissipated by his heirs. Starling was the only one of the four men whose continued presence and steady prosperity continued to contribute to the development of Columbus through its formative decades.

Columbus had proved its hardiness and ability to survive under the whiplash of adversity during those rugged years of beginning. In spite of the high toll exacted by disease, and despite the losses suffered in economic slumps, the capital carried on and dug in against the worst, hardly daring to hope for the better days that were almost immediately ahead.

# The Way Out of the Wilderness:
## 1825 to 1835

THE ADVANCE MAN for prosperity and a higher level of civilization arrived in sickness-beset, wilderness-isolated Columbus on October 5, 1825. His name was Jonathan Knight, a United States commissioner who had been charged with conducting a survey of a section of the wilderness route from the old state capital at Zanesville to Columbus, a distance of some fifty-five miles.

A pioneer road, Zane's Trace, already ran through the area, but something better than that rude road was obviously needed. A better highway would be of inestimable importance to the development of Central Ohio—and, of course, to the capital city. The vitally-needed section of the National Road (later designated as U.S. 40) was completed in 1833, and its effect on Columbus could not be overestimated. The town at once became a key community, a crossroads center on the most important highway leading to the as yet unopened American West.

Shortly after the opening of the National Road link, Columbus became a city. The town that had been laid out in a forested plot in 1812 and which had been incorporated as a borough in 1816, reached city status in 1834. Its incorporation by act of the legislature took place on March 3, 1834.

The borough stage had been an interesting one. Until 1816, the capital's affairs had been controlled and regulated by the general laws of the state. By that time, however, the population had grown to 700 people and the legislature felt Columbus should begin to govern itself. The corporate authority of the borough was vested in nine councilmen elected directly by the citizens. The councilmen, in turn, elected a mayor, recorder, and treasurer from their own ranks, with the mayor serving as ex-officio president of the council.

Columbus Inn was the scene of the first election on May 6, 1816. A week later, on May 13, the newly elected members of the council met and organized the borough's first municipal government. The councilmen were Robert W. McCoy, John Cutler, Robert Armstrong, Henry Brown, Caleb Houston, Michael Patton, Jeremiah Armstrong, Jarvis Pike, and John Kerr. The first administrative officials of the new borough were Jarvis Pike, mayor; R. W. McCoy, recorder; Samuel King, marshal; Robert Armstrong, treasurer; John Kerr, surveyor; and William Long, clerk of the market.

Growth was the immediate order of the day in the borough. The population of 700 had swollen to a count of 1,450 in 1820. A decade later, in 1830, there were 2,437 residents. Between 1830 and 1840, the dual stimuli, the National Road and the Ohio-Erie Canal, had an electrifying effect on the growth of Columbus, and the number of residents almost tripled in number during that period to a total of 6,048 by 1840.

Under the terms of the enactment of incorporation in 1834, the city was divided into three wards: Ward 1 embraced all the municipality north of State Street; Ward 2 included all the territory between State and Rich streets; and Ward 3 took in all the city south of Rich Street. Each ward was to be represented by four councilmen, with one new councilman to be elected annually from each ward. The mayor was to serve a two-year term. All other municipal officers were to be appointed by the council.

The first city election held under the new charter was on April 14, 1834. John Brooks was elected the city's first mayor. City councilmen elected in that history first polling included Henry Brown, Otis Crosby, Robert McCoy, Joseph Ridgway, Sr., all of Ward 1; William Long, Jonathan Neeramer, Francis Stewart, and Noah H. Swayne, representing Ward 3. Robert W. McCoy, a member of the borough council since its organization in 1816, was chosen as the first president of the new city council. He continued in that office through successive re-elections until his resignation in July 1853. He served as a councilman for 37 years altogether.

If the National Road had opened Columbus to land travel, another vital development, the Ohio-Erie Canal, was to give the capital a water connection with the outside world. The great canal connecting Cleveland on Lake Erie with Portsmouth on the Ohio River was still under construction in 1827 when work was begun on the digging of a lateral branch that would make Columbus part of the waterway.

On September 13, 1831, water first flowed into the connecting canal at Lockbourne. Two days later, the first boat, the *Governor Brown*, arrived from Circleville. It was a red-letter date—the opening of a new era in the brief history of Columbus. Travelers and cargoes for the first time could move by boat from the capital to the Great Lakes or the Ohio River. Either water route, if pursued, led to the Atlantic Ocean and the rest of the world.

In the beginning, only a few years before, the principal means of travel in and out of the new capital had been by foot, by horseback, or by wagon. The going continued to be rough, even after civilization had advanced to the point of road building. The first real link between Columbus and the outside world was a modest one, but very important. It was a toll bridge across the Scioto River to Franklinton. It was built in 1816 by Lucas Sullivant, a pioneer surveyor who had founded Franklinton in 1797. Sullivant, a remarkable man in every way and a natural leader, had been engaged at that time to survey lands and to locate land warrants in the Virginia Military District, west of the Scioto River. In August

1797 he laid out a new settlement at what he called the "fork of the Scioto," and named it in honor of Benjamin Franklin.

That, in a real sense, was the beginning of Columbus, because Sullivant's settlement in time became an integral part of the capital city, and Sullivant himself became one of its leading citizens.

Hardly anything occurred in Franklinton that did not involve Sullivant and his multiple talents. He built the first court house in 1807-08 and became the president of the first bank, organized in 1816. Then, when he built the bridge across the Scioto in 1816, he hammered the first link in the eventual union of Franklinton and Columbus.

The history of Franklinton as an independent community was short, but it did have one glorious highlight. After the outbreak of the War of 1812, it was selected as an important troop mobilization center, becoming the frontier headquarters of the command of Gen. William Henry Harrison. But the town's fortunes went into decline after the war as the state capital across the river asserted its dominance. The coup de grace came about in 1824, when Columbus was chosen to replace Franklinton as the seat of Franklin County.

The older town, stripped of its honors, became dependent upon Columbus and receded into the shadows, lapsing into the role of a pleasant old neighborhood with an interesting past.

EVEN THOUGH THE TOWN was only twenty years old at the time, Columbus already was the subject of some fanciful art work, as exemplified by this ceramic platter dating back to 1832. There wasn't too much similarity between the crude little village and the picture on the plate, but the flattery was no doubt well received. (OHS)

MANY DESIGNS were submitted for the proposed new capitol building of Ohio in the late 1830s, including the two shown here. The final plan was a combination of designs, but the influence of the one whose west front elevation is shown *(above)* may be readily seen. (CC-J)

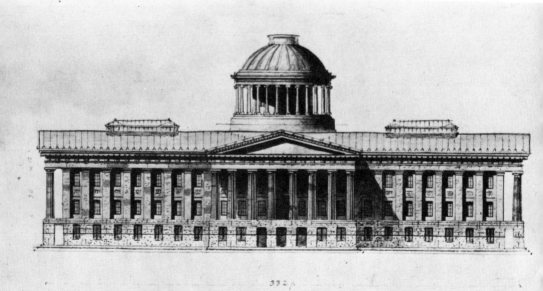

FIRST PREMIUM DESIGN FOR THE CAPITOL OF OHIO, AT COLUMBUS. BY WALTER. OF CINCINNATI.

# The End of the Beginning: 1835 to 1860

THE MIDDLE of the nineteenth century was one of the most remarkable periods in American history in terms of human progress. Columbus shared in the forward lunge of civilization and drew strength from all the major developments of the time.

The growing capital city hardly had time to accustom itself to the advantages brought about by the building of new roads and the marvelous canal system when, in February 1850, the first railroad train puffed its way into the city. The following month marked the beginning of regular passenger train service between Columbus and Cincinnati.

Within an incredibly short period of time, the strategic geographical position of the young city asserted itself dramatically as it became a rail center of national importance. In time it would become the hub of seven trunk railroads with 18 divisions connecting it with all parts of the United States. At the peak of the railroad age, some seventy passenger trains would serve the city every day, not to mention the fleets of nine interurban rail lines that would, presently, fan out from the city to provide matchless regional rail transportation.

Progress always demands a price, of course, and in the case of Columbus the arrival of the railroads had a ruinous effect on two other forms of transportation which hardly had had time to become well established. One was the canal system, the other the system of coach travel.

The first stage coach service through Columbus, carrying passengers and mail, had begun in 1816. It ran once a week between Columbus and Chillicothe. In the next ten years new coach lines were established between the capital and communities all over the state. By 1831, some seventy stage coaches rolled into Columbus every week. That form of highway transportation continued to grow, connecting Columbus not only with other cities and towns in the state but also providing interstate transportation. Thanks to the city's strategic location and excellent facilities, it became the staging area in the late 1840s for the westward dash of thousands of Forty-niners. Conestoga wagon trains rumbled through the streets day and night.

Rail travel was infinitely faster and more comfortable than the highway coaches, of course, and the public was quick to switch to train travel as soon as it became available. In 1853, when the Ohio Stage Company sold its equipment for use out west, it still had fifty coaches operating out of Columbus. But that was the end of the line for one of the most picturesque forms of transportation that the country had ever seen.

Travel by canal boat continued until after the Civil War, but its decline and death were inevitable in the face of rail competition. Canals as freight carriers continued, nevertheless, to serve a useful role as regulators of rail rates by providing a competing form of transportation. There can be no denying, though, the importance of the canals in the development and growth of Columbus. During the period in which the Ohio-Erie Canal was in its full use, from 1831 to mid-century, a mere twenty years, the population of Columbus grew at a steady pace—from 2,437 in 1830 to 17,882 in 1850. The same rate of growth prevailed in the decade that followed, taking Columbus to a total of 18,554 population in 1860, just before the outbreak of the Civil War.

More impressive than mere numbers was the change in the physical look of Columbus during that growth period from 1830 to 1860. During this time, the city lost its primitive pioneer appearance and began to take on the image of a state capital. The center piece in this transformation was, of course, the capitol building itself.

The first State House had been built by the syndicate of developers in 1814 in accordance with the founding agreement with the state government. Its site was the southwest corner of the Public Square. It was of modest dimensions, but built of bricks—some of which, ironically enough, had been made from the clay taken from the impressive prehistoric Indian mound, the tomb of numerous skeletons, that stood at the southwest corner of Mound Street and High. The state, at any rate, got its full money's worth in that original capitol because the sturdy stone-and-brick structure stood and served well until it was destroyed by fire on a Sunday morning, April 1, 1852.

The state government had actually outgrown the building many years before, and plans to replace it with a more adequate structure for the times had been underway for years before the fire, but there had been complications that delayed the project. Authorization for construction of a new State House in the Public Square had been given by the legislature as early as January 26, 1838, and the cornerstone had been laid on July 4, 1839. During the rest of that summer considerable work was done on the foundation of the new building. But a political feud prevented work from being resumed next spring. Mixed in with the political issues was a growing resentment toward Columbus itself and the advantages it enjoyed as the capital of Ohio.

A member of the legislature from Cuyahoga County, William B. Lloyd, had come under investigation, and some of his colleagues in the House of Representatives voted to censure him. But some friends of Lloyd in Columbus, 63 mostly young men, expressed their confidence in his integrity and pledged their support in an advertisement that appeared in the *Ohio State Journal* of February 17, 1840. The members of the legislature who had voted against Lloyd took such offense at this publication that on the following day they introduced into the House a bill repealing the act authorizing erection of the new State House. It passed both houses and became law on March 10, 1840.

THE GREAT COVERED BRIDGE that once linked Columbus and Franklinton, the rival town on the west bank of the Scioto River, was one of the marvelous achievements of the early nineteenth century. It carried Broad Street traffic across the river. (CD)

More than six years were to pass before work on the new capitol would be resumed. Columbus, meanwhile, had to defend itself against the attacks of those who chose at that time to propose moving the seat of state government to a different site. Their drive was unsuccessful, but it was not beaten back entirely until the spring of 1843.

In February 1846, a second act to provide for the erection of a new State House was passed by the legislature. Work was not resumed, however, until 1848. The legislative halls were finally ready for use by January 1, 1857, even though the building was not completed until 1859—twenty years after construction had begun.

No single architect can claim credit for the design of the new State House. More than fifty plans had been volunteered by architects in the United States in response to a national appeal by Ohio authorities. Three of those plans were selected for consideration, and the author of one of them, Henry Walter of Cincinnati, was hired to supervise the construction of a building that was, in reality, a blend of ideas. The choice of design was controversial then and continued to be argued through the years, although its massive dignity in the classic Doric style also has drawn widespread admiration.

The dimensions of the State House are most impressive. It is 304 feet long and 184 feet wide. Its height, from the rotunda floor to the top of the truncated dome, is 136 feet. It features eight massive stone columns on the east and west fronts, and four columns each on the north and south sides. The main entrance is on the west side of the building. It is said to be the largest building of its kind in the United States outside of the national Capitol in Washington, D.C.. Its cost was $1,350,000. Appropriately, the gray limestone for the new building was home-grown, taken from a quarry on the Scioto River just west of the city. One of the reasons for the low cost of the structure was the use of convict labor, courtesy of the Ohio State Penitentiary.

Undoubtedly the most controversial aspect of the otherwise magnificent new capitol was the truncated design of the dome which gave the building a flat-top look that would very soon be compared unfavorably with the look of the first iron-clad navy vessel, the *Monitor*. It left the State House with an unfinished look because high, rounded domes were the traditional tops of capitol buildings. But there were those, then as now, who said the flat look was classier. Nevertheless, the state has ever since been busy denying that a rounded dome was stricken from the plans as an economy measure.

The first governor to occupy the new State House was Gov. Salmon P. Chase, who a few years later filled the post of Secretary of the Treasury in the cabinet of Pres. Abraham Lincoln and then went on to become the distinguished Chief Justice of the United States Supreme Court.

Nobody could mistake the tremendous significance implicit in the construction of the grand new edifice to house the instruments of Ohio government in the young capital city. It stood out as a symbol of the end of the rude, rough beginning and the start of a fresh, more sophisticated era for both city and state. The people of Columbus looked at the magnificent State House with glowing pride and undisguised wonder. It didn't seem possible to those who had been around from the beginning that their city could have advanced to such heights from a clearing in the forest fastness over a mere 44 years, but there stood the majestic proof in the center of the capital.

[ 22 ]

CAPITAL UNIVERSITY was the first institution of higher learning in Columbus. This is an artist's depiction of the university building that stood at High and Goodale from 1850 to 1876. (CC-J)

ONE OF THE EARLIEST known photographs of Columbus is this indistinct but historic picture of Broad and High streets in 1849, when, purportedly, a crowd of westbound pioneers had gathered to begin their trek to California, then in the grip of the Gold Rush. The adventurers are mounted on horses while many spectators mill in the street intersection. (CD)

EVOLUTION OF THE RAIL TERMINALS: The first railroad station *(above)* in Columbus was the barn-like structure on the left. It was built in 1850 and demolished a mere twenty-five years later to make way for a grander terminal. Notice the horse-drawn streetcar (left) and the lineup of horse-drawn buggies (upper right) waiting for passengers to alight. A stagecoach is among the vehicles standing by for customers. The successor to this first station *(left)* was the four-story depot on the right, constructed in 1875. The larger number of tracks, as well as the heightened grandeur of the terminal itself, tell the story of the fantastic growth in rail travel in the 25-year period from 1850 to 1875. Finally, below, there is the third Union Station, acclaimed as one of the finest in the United States in its heyday. (OHS)

SIMON LAZARUS *(inset)*. an immigrant who arrived in Columbus with his family in 1851, was the founder of the nationally-known Lazarus Department Store. The beginnings were modest in this one-room store in a building at the southwest corner of Town and High streets. The sign on the Town Street side identifies the store as "The Square Dealing Clothier." When the founder died in 1877, he was succeeded by his sons Fred and Ralph, whose initials still adorn the name of the giant F. & R. Lazarus & Company Department Store. (Burke/Bell)

[ 25 ]

LONG BEFORE the Deshler-Wallick Hotel came to occupy the northwest corner of Broad and High, another hotel sat on the site. It was the old St. Charles Hotel, depicted here by an artist of the mid-nineteenth century. (CD)

AN OLD, OLD PHOTO of downtown Columbus, possibly dating back to the 1850s, is this shot of the southwest corner of State and High. The leaning gas lamp light, relatively new to the street scene, and the quagmire that passed for a street, tell their story of the times. (OHS)

# War and Peace: 1860 to 1890

NO STATE in the Union was more fully represented in the Civil War than Ohio; not only by the thousands of men from the Buckeye State who served in uniform in the Union ranks, but also by the leaders in the national administration and on the battlefield. Ohioans were prominent at all levels.

In a famous monument on the state-house grounds, erected after the war, Levi Schofield of Cleveland, the designer, tells part of the remarkable story. The monument is surmounted by a bronze effigy of the Roman matron, Cornelia, who stands with outstretched hands while at her feet are chiseled her classic words: "These are my jewels." The names of some of the famous Ohioans who rose to fame through their service in the Civil War follow: Gen. Ulysses S. Grant, Gen. William Tecumseh Sherman, Gen. Phillip H. Sheridan, Secretary of War Edwin Stanton, Secretary of the Treasury Salmon P. Chase, Gen. James A. Garfield, and Gen. Rutherford B. Hayes. It was a truly remarkable group of men for any single state to contribute; three of them went on to the ultimate national honor, the presidency, and one became chief justice of the United States Supreme Court.

Just as Franklinton had served as a mobilization center for the frontier forces in the War of 1812, Columbus became a Union Army center in the Civil War. Goodale Park became Camp Jackson, designated as the rendezvous camp for all Ohio troops north of Hamilton County and south of the Western Reserve. Camp Thomas was established east of the Worthington plank road, three or four miles north of Columbus. An arsenal was built that became, in time, Fort Hayes. Camp Jackson was set up on the National Road, four or five miles west of the city. Its name shortly thereafter was changed to Camp Chase in honor of the ex-governor. While it was the scene of active recruiting and training for service, it achieved more lasting fame, or notoriety, as one sees it, as the site of a prison for Confederate soldiers captured in battle.

CREASED AND BLOTCHED by time and ill use, this old and rare photograph *(above)* is still of considerable importance because it allows a peek over the stockade fence of Camp Chase, where Confederate soldiers were imprisoned and died by the thousands during the Civil War. Another rare picture of the camp *(below)* shows a sweeping view of the tragic place. A memorial marker *(left)* was later erected honoring the dead soldiers. (OHS/Bell)

The tragedy of Camp Chase is to be found in the cemetery that it left behind. Disease rampant in the camp was able to do what Union firearms had not—it killed 2,260 Confederate prisoners in the wartime prison. All but a few still lie buried there.

The war came home to the people of Columbus more directly when Confederate raider John Morgan invaded Ohio and caused near-panic before he and his men were captured in Columbiana County. All 71 of the raiders were brought to Columbus and confined to the Ohio Penitentiary in October 1863. Less than two months later, Morgan and six of his captains made their escape, causing considerable embarassment to the prison authorities.

Ohio was a pivotal state in Civil War days, and Columbus was a capital city of high national importance. Abraham Lincoln had visited the city to make his first important address in Ohio on September 16, 1859. His next visit was as a martyr. A train brought Lincoln's body to Columbus on April 29, 1865. His coffin, resting on a dais in a hearse, rode through the city from Union Station to the Capitol. There, on a catafalque in the rotunda, it remained on public view all day long. Thousands of mourners from all parts of the state crowded the city center to pay their last tribute.

The war years seemed to give impetus to the city's growth. Where the population previously had grown at a modest but steady rate, the head count suddenly jumped approximately 70%, from 18,554 in 1860 to 31,274 by 1870. There was furious building activity as the city tried to keep pace with the swollen numbers. Commerce and industry leaped forward at war's end. Six new banking houses and the first building and loan company were organized. Manufacturing generally remained on the light side, but there was a spectacular expansion in buggy manufacturing. By 1880, more than twenty companies in Columbus were building twenty thousand vehicles for a world-wide market.

Horse-drawn streetcar service was inaugurated, giving the streets a big-city look; even more gratifying to most residents was the building of the first water works and the seemingly miraculous delivery of unlimited quantities of water directly to the homes.

The first streetcar line went into operation on High Street with a one-horse, single-track system that ran, in the beginning, from Union Station to the Court House at Mound Street, aided no end by the fact that High Street had become the city's first paved street in 1867.

A new City Hall, called "one of the most beautiful and imposing public edifices that adorn the capital," rose on State Street, nearly opposite the southern entrance of the Capitol building. Work on it was begun in May 1869, and it was opened to public use on March 28, 1872. Its cost was $175,000.

Street lights that burned coal oil were installed at important street intersections. A new theatrical palace, the Opera House, completed in 1864, also brightened the downtown scene, as did the Atheneum, the former State Street Theater which had been rebuilt by William A. Neil and given a new name when it was opened in November 1871; he was the same Neil, by the way, whose family name was memorialized by the city's oldest hotel, the Neil House, which traced its beginnings to 1822.

An event of lasting significance to Columbus was the opening, on September 7, 1873, of the Ohio Agricultural and Mechanical College, an institution made possible by federal

ON THE 29TH OF APRIL, 1865, fifteen days after the assassination of Abraham Lincoln in Washington, the funeral train bearing the President's body came to Columbus via Cleveland. Five divisions of troops formed what was called "the most impressive and imposing procession ever seen in Columbus." The coffin of the martyred President was on display in the Capitol rotunda from early morning until evening, and uncounted thousands of Ohioans filed past the catafalque. This old lithograph depicts the Lincoln funeral cortege as it made its way east on Broad Street. (OHS)

ALL SET FOR ACTION, wrenches and lamps in hand, were these men who constituted the entire service department of the Columbus Gas & Fuel Company in 1865. (CGS)

subsidy in the form of land grants. This forerunner of Ohio State University had one building, University Hall, and somewhere between thirty and forty students when it began. It also had 327 acres of land, the former Neil farm. By 1891, it could boast of five buildings, with three more under construction.

Higher education had come to Columbus earlier, it is true, in the form of Capital University, which had been founded as a seminary in 1831 by the Evangelical Lutheran Synod. At first, it occupied a fourteen-acre site at the southern limit of High Street, moved to Town and Fifth streets in 1849, then to the northwest corner of High and Goodale in 1853, and finally, in 1876, to its campus on the National Road, on Main Street.

Another religion-affiliated institution, Saint Mary's of the Springs, similarly predated Ohio State. It was established in Columbus in 1866 by the Dominican Sisters from Somerset, Perry County.

Industrial cities count their progress statistically in terms of dollars and production capacity. Columbus was not without industry, but that was a minor part of the civic scene. Politics, government, transportation, business, and education were the pillars on which the city rested as the nineteenth century moved into its final decade.

There had been another forward leap in population between 1870 and 1880, taking the city to a total count of 51,647. The boom continued unabated, so that Columbus had, by 1890, a population of 88,150.

These census figures seemed incredible to the oldtimers who had known the capital for a long time but, as fantastic as the city's development had been, Columbus was teetering on the edge of an even more glorious period of growth. The best was yet to be.

[ 31 ]

ONE BLEAK DAY IN 1868 some laddies of the Columbus Fire Department posed with an impressive piece of horse-drawn equipment for a pioneer photographer. There's no explaining the showoff on the slanty roof of the shed in the right background. (CC-J)

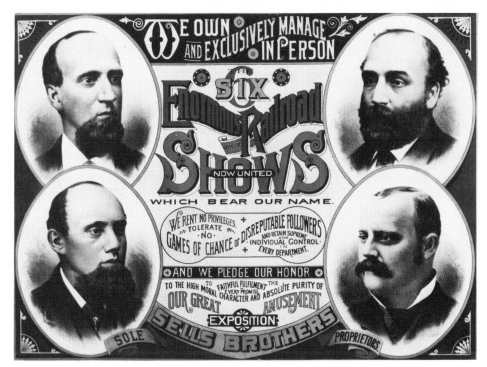

COLUMBUS WAS HOME to the famous Sells Brothers Citcus, one of America's largest traveling entertainment units after the Civil War all the way into the twentieth century. In its advanced years, it was
known as the Sells Brothers-Floto Circus. The four Sells brothers are shown on this old show poster
that goes to great and eloquent length to affirm the purity of the circus product. (Weisheimer)

THE ACADEMY of Saint Mary of the Springs, a college for women on Johnstown Road in Sunbury
on the east side of Columbus, dates back to September 1866, when it was created by the Dominican
Sisters. The picturesque farm site, donated to the order by Theodore Leonard of Columbus, has many
ground springs. (CPL)

REGIMENTATION at the Ohio Penitentiary in 1868: The prisoners marched in lock-step and wore the horizontally striped uniforms that told the world that they were felons. (OHS)

AN UNSTEADY LOOKING FRAME BUILDING at 170 North High in 1872 housed an interesting assortment of enterprises and almost as much of a variety of human beings anxious to pose in front. The Emporium of Natural History used the upper story, while the street level was shared by R. David's Variety Store and the Union Pacific Tea Company. It appears that a 2 x 4 is propping up the Variety Store's front. A vending machine, perhaps for popcorn, stands in front of the doorway. (CD)

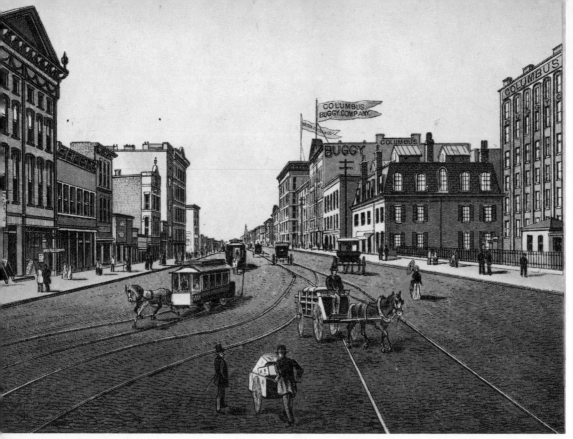

A POSTCARD MEMORIALIZES the early High Street scene, probably in the 1870s, looking south from Union Depot. The pennants are flying from the roof of the famous Columbus Buggy Company. (CC-J)

[ 34 ] THE COURT HOUSE EXCHANGE about 1875 was also known as the Schrimer Building. Notice the wash hanging out on the line, the huckster's wagon (lower left), the Keystone-style Kops (left of center), the casual poses of the people on the veranda, and the elegant coach in the street below. (CD)

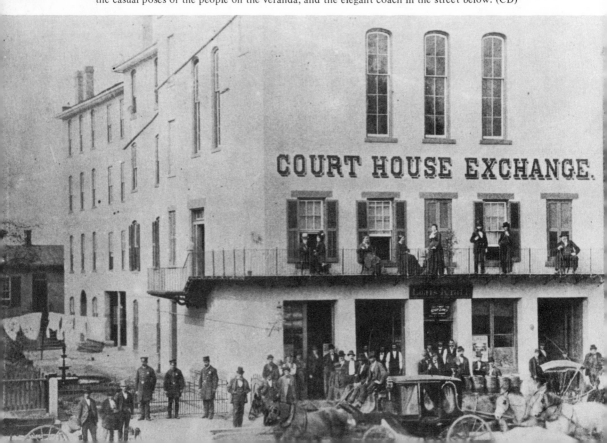

A FAMILIAR BUILDING to generations of Columbus residents was the old Bank Block, shown here, a ginger-bread laden creation of 1878. It stood at the southeast corner of Long and High. It was also known as the Sessions Bank Block. (CD)

THE FIRST BUILDING of Capital University in its new location in Bexley was Lehmann Hall, the university's administration building, built in 1876. (CU)

THE DOCKING BASIN for canal boats in Columbus in the 1870s or 1880s. The basin was just south of Main Street. The canal was abandoned about 1912. (OHS)

NO FOLLY, IT SEEMS, was Ziegfeld's store in Columbus back in the old days—1880, according to the records. C. G. Ziegfeld & Son's Vienna Bakery and Confectionery apparently did a rather brisk business, judging from the ten-member staff that stood out in front of the store to pose for the photographer on that distant day. (CD)

THE CITY MARKET HOUSE as it appeared in the 1870s or 1880s. The site of the market was Town Street and South Fourth Street. (OHS)

THE FIRST PRESIDENT of Ohio State University was Prof. Edward Orton of Yellow Springs, Ohio, a teacher of geology, mining, and metallurgy. He was hired as both chief administrator and full professor. He resigned as president in June 1881, but continued as professor of geology. His service is memorialized by Orton Hall, seat of the Department of Geology, constructed in 1892. (OSU)

THE YEAR WAS 1877 and the gentlemen casually lolling by the waterside, all six of them, represented the entire OSU Class of 1878. At least one of them, judging by the uniform, must have gotten stuck with R.O.T.C. (OSU)

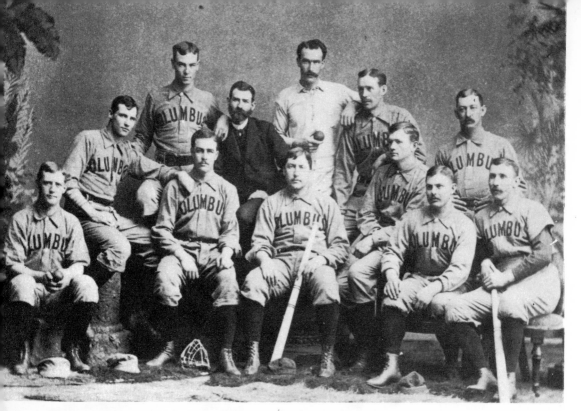

THE SPORT usually associated with Columbus is football, but professional baseball was popular long before the OSU football teams captured the hearts of the people. Here is one of the teams that represented Columbus in the professional leagues in the nineteenth century. (OHS)

PHOTOGRAPHY was still a novelty in 1884 and it was the custom for business establishments occasionally to submit to this kind of group picture of the proprietor and the sales staff and office help. This is the German Furniture Company and its people. Judging from some of the street samples, including the fancy baby carriage (left), products made of wicker were all the vogue that year. (Lazarus)

NOT EVEN THE RAINY WEATHER could dampen the enthusiasm of the people who turned out in 1885 for the ceremonial cornerstone laying *(above)* at the site of the new, about-to-be-built Franklin County Court House at the corner of Mound Street and South High. When it was finished, it was the pride of all the people. The truly magnificent building *(below)* was dedicated on July 13, 1887, and cost, including a boiler house and equipment, $470,000. (Lazarus/CLP)

COLUMBUS was not much older than photography itself in 1888—a time of horse-drawn streetcars, buggies, cobblestones, primitive street lighting, and bicycles—when peace seemed to pervade all the things that were. It was as if the city were too young to worry about the shortcomings of life itself and had arrived at a nice harmonious arrangement with fate. (CPL)

EAST BROAD STREET, sometime shortly after the end of the Civil War. Notice the Conestoga-type wagons in the immediate foreground. Residences still crowd the street just east of the Board of Trade Building. One of the homes was rented by Pres. Rutherford B. Hayes and his family when he was serving as governor of Ohio. The office was just a quick dash across Broad Street. (CPL)

STATE INSTITUTIONS of great size and grandeur sprung up almost simultaneously in Columbus during and after the Civil War as Ohio established itself as possibly the most progressive state in the Union in the care and treatment of unfortunates. The State Asylum for the Blind, authorized by the Ohio legislature in 1869, followed the institutional architecture of the day. It is shown here about 1888. It stands at Parsons and Main. In the later years, it was taken over for the use of the Ohio State Department of Highway Safety. (CPL)

WHEN THE OLD FEDERAL BUILDING WAS NEW, the corner of State and Third streets was a serene intersection. If the building itself looks disturbingly different, it is because its size was doubled in later years. It was a magnificent new addition to downtown Columbus, though, when this picture was taken sometime in the 1880s. (CPL)

THE STATE ASYLUM FOR THE INSANE in Columbus, shown in 1888, was the largest institution of its kind in the world when it was built. Construction was started in 1870 and took seven years to completion in 1877. It replaced an asylum built in 1835-39 which was destroyed by fire on November 18, 1868. Gov. Rutherford B. Hayes laid the cornerstone of the new institutional facility located two miles west of the State House on 300 acres of land off West Broad Street. Cost of the enormous building was $1½ million. The distance around its outside wall was 1¼ miles. (CPL)

AMONG THE ELEGANT RESIDENCES in Columbus during the latter half of the nineteenth century were the homes of Thomas E. Powell *(top)*, George M. Peters *(center)*, and Henry M. Neil *(bottom)*. The Neil house on Indianola Avenue near Fifteenth Avenue was later remodeled and became the Kappa Sigma Fraternity house of Ohio State University. (CPL)

THE PARK HOTEL and the Columbus Savings Bank occupied the corner of North High and Goodale when this picture was snapped sometime, it is believed, in the 1880s. The view is north from Goodale. A horse-drawn streetcar is approaching down High Street (to the right). (CPL)

ONE OF THE UNUSUAL EVENTS in Columbus during the encampment of the Grand Army of the Republic in the capital in 1888 was this straw parade through the streets. (Lazarus)

CITY HALL in the 1880s stood on East Street, the later site of the Ohio Theater. (Lazarus)

WHEN THE BUGGY WAS KING, the Buckeye Buggy Company of Columbus was one of the world's largest manufacturers of the horse-drawn vehicle. (OHS)

EVERYBODY ASSOCIATED WITH an early Columbus financial institutions, the Rhinehard Bank, posed for this street photograph one fine day—sometime, probably, in the 1880s or 1890s. The man with the Fu Manchu mustache and the Napoleonic pose in the center may have been Rhinehard himself. (OHS)

A NETWORK OF STREETS, overpasses, and tunnels sprang into being near the Union Station to accommodate the trains and vehicular traffic. This rare 1888 view shows the tunnel than ran under High Street. Among the vehicles on the street, lower left, is an interesting version of the stagecoach. The plant of the Buckeye Buggy Company is directly in the background, hardly visible through the heavy layer of smoke that blanketed the city as a normal, everyday fact of life in the early days of the industrial revolution. (OHS)

THE ORIGINAL HOME of the *Columbus Dispatch* was this small building at the corner of High Street and Lynn Alley, shown in the 1880s. (CD)

THE OLD NEIL HOUSE hotel is just left of center, on the corner of the alley, in this 1880s view of High Street. The old Huntington Bank is on the corner, extreme right. The Neil House shown was built in 1861 and served until it was replaced by the present Neil House in 1925. (Burke)

A COLUMBUS MERCHANT, Paul Mone, whose store was on Spring Street, posed with his employees and relatives in this 1880s photograph. Even the baby got in the act. (CD)

A NINETEENTH-CENTURY ASTRO-dome? Looking astonishingly similar to one of today's superstructures is this domed auditorium called the Colosseum, built in 1880 for the Ohio centennial celebrations on the fairgrounds in Columbus. This fantastic glimpse of tomorrow seated 10,000 persons. (CD)

THE OLD UNION DEPOT, built in 1874, was still in useful service sometime between 1880 and 1889. Among the interesting features of the picture are the horse-drawn passenger conveyance to the right of the building and the solitary figure of a man standing on the roof of the building, just above and to the right of the letters spelling out "Union Depot." (CD)

[ 48 ]

THE FIRST BUILDING of Ohio State University, which began as the Ohio Agricultural and Mechanical College, was University Hall. Classes were first held in this building on September 7, 1873, even before construction work had been completed. The site of the university was the Neil Farm, lying on the Worthington Road about two miles north of Columbus. Designer of the first building was Jacob Snyder of Akron. (CPL)

THE PRINTING PRESSES were stilled one day in the 1880s at the J. W. Martin Printing shop just long enough to permit management and employees to pose for the photographer. Vests and derbies and mustaches were de rigeur in those days. (CD)

CONDUCTOR MARION O. CLARK, on the boarding step of this air-conditioned horse-drawn street-car, stopped one summer day in 1888 in front of old Northwood School. It was on the High Street line serving the Union Depot and North Columbus. The identity of the motorman is not known.

NO SIGHT in the old days was more dramatic than a horse-drawn fire engine racing to answer an alarm. This troika combination was caught in action about 1888. (OHS)

DROP A
NICKEL
IN THE SLOT
AND SECURE A
BEAU
FOR
SATURDAY NIGHT

F. & R. LAZARUS & CO.,
STRICTLY ONE PRICE
CLOTHING, BOOTS, SHOES, HATS AND FURNISHING GOODS,
Cor. High and Town Sts. COLUMBUS, O.

ESCORT SERVICES still were far in the future when the Lazarus Store came up with this humorous advertisement about 1889. (OHS)

IT ISN'T LIKELY that the cupboard of this Hubbard family home was ever bare. It was one of the loveliest residences in Columbus in its nineteenth-century time of glory, the pride of the near north side. The home was built at the corner of Hubbard Avenue and High Street in 1850 by William B. Hubbard. The architect was Richard A. Sheldon, who later designed Starling Medical College, later Saint Francis Hospital. (CD)

# Peace and War: 1890 to 1920

COLUMBUS HAD TAKEN ON a metropolitan look as the Victorian era came to a close. The capital in 1891 was not only a nationally important political center that drew famous visitors and statesmen, but it had become a busy, bustling place in its own capacity as a city.

Columbus lies athwart some of the world's richest farming country, and it was the natural market place and the place for transshipment for the produce that the agricultural heartland of Ohio yielded. It had also become, quite naturally, a banking and commercial center of Central Ohio. Just as it had served as a crossroads of wilderness traffic during its pioneer years, Columbus became a business crossroads as it grew to maturity. The reason was the same—key location. The wealth of the farm country and the output of the tremendous Appalachian coal fields just to the south and east came together in Columbus, joining the oil and gas to the northwest and the clay deposits that abounded in the Central Ohio region. All those vital ingredients, put together in the proper mix, made for success.

The outbreak of the Spanish-American War in 1898 put Columbus on a war footing again, emphasizing its strategic site in times of emergency. This time, the army established a 500-acre mobilization and training center called Camp Bushnell on East Broad Street, beyond Bexley.

The week of August 26, 1912, was a special week in Columbus history because it was the time set aside for the celebration of the city's one-hundredth anniversary. It was celebrated in conjunction with the Ohio State Fair, and the highlight of the celebration was Pres. William Howard Taft's speech at the Fair Grounds.

Just a few months later, in the spring of 1913, the city's west side—old Franklinton, the town that had been passed by in the search for a capital site because it was flood-susceptible lowland—was devastated by the worst flood in Columbus history. Some 93 persons lost their lives, thousands were isolated in their homes for three or four days, and

END OF THE BEGINNING: Franklin County had outgrown the facilities offered by the first County Court House and its annex (built in 1840 and 1852 respectively) by the time the 1880s rolled around. Voters approved a $500,000 bond issue for a new Court House on the same site in the spring of 1884. Shortly thereafter the historic Court House and its companion building were demolished. This rare photograph from the Baker Art Gallery shows the dismantling underway. Notice the mob scene on the roof of the Court House. (Weisheimer)

life on the west side of the Scioto River was completely disrupted for many weeks. Property damage was estimated at $5,622,000. The number of private dwellings flooded was 4,071. Many of the homes were reduced to tinderwood by the raging waters. But the disaster led to long-needed flood control measures to protect the city in the future. Levees, retaining walls, and the great O'Shaughnessy Dam on the Scioto River 12 miles north of the city, were built.

World War I again brought the city back to its familiar role as a mobilization and training center for the army, with troops funneled through Fort Hayes, the processing center, and with the State Fair Grounds commandeered for army purposes. One of the most famous heroes to emerge from the war was a Columbus son, Eddie Rickenbacker, who had achieved a measure of prominence before the war as an automobile race driver. Downing 27 enemy planes. he became America's leading air ace, and thus a national hero. Meanwhile, a daughter of Columbus, Elsie Janis (Bierbower), drew the nation's plaudits for her indefatigable contribution as an entertainer of the soldiers on the battle fronts in France.

When the war ended, Columbus settled back into the pleasant contentment that had become characteristic of life in Ohio's capital city. Much of the stress and strain that had gone with the dynamic growth of the sixty-year period from 1860 to 1920 disappeared after the war, and a time of stabilization set in. An army on the march has to halt once in a while, or at least slow its pace, until it has consolidated its lines of supply and gathered new strength for future advances.

In that sixty-year period, Columbus had gone from a population of 18,554 to 125,560 in 1900; to 181,511 in 1910; and then on to 237,031 in 1920. The village cocoon had burst wide open, revealing a small metropolis, very pretty, but unsure of itself.

THE NEAR WEST SIDE, old Franklinton, had become something of an urban mess by the time the city moved into the 1890s. Plans to renovate the old neighborhood and make for a more beautiful approach to the capitol, seen in the distance, left of center, were a subject of discussion even in that early day. This old photograph shows the view from the west side of the Scioto River, looking east, from a point somewhere around Starling Street, sometime before 1900 (Weisheimer)

GOODALE PARK about 1890 was, by contrast, a scenic beauty and one of the most popular recreational centers in Columbus in the late nineteenth century and subsequent decades. (OHS)

THE WORST FIRE IN COLUMBUS HISTORY at the time was the one that destroyed the Chittenden Hotel, Chittenden Hall, and two theaters, the Henrietta and the Park, on the night of November 24, 1893. The complex was so new that it, indeed, was still under construction. (CD)

THE CAR BARN of the Columbus Central Railway Company in 1890 looked like an Oriental mosque. Streetcars in those days carried more than passengers, as the stacked milk cans to the left tell us. (CD)

COLUMBUS CENTRAL RAILWAY
COMPANY 1890

SAINT ANTHONY'S HOSPITAL on the east side at Hawthorne and St. Claire, built in 1890, was one of the largest in Columbus at the turn of the century. (OHS)

SAINT PATRICK'S Catholic Church at Grant and Naughton streets, built in 1855, was known as the "Irish Church of Columbus." It is shown here in 1890. (Burke)

THE RESIDENCE of the bishop of the Columbus Catholic Diocese was this home on East Broad Street, shown in this 1890 photograph. The house to the immediate left was the old Deshler residence. It later was purchased by the Catholic diocese. (Burke)

THE WYANDOTTE BUILDING on West Broad Street, close to High, is one of the hardiest survivors of the early years in downtown Columbus. It is the tall building in the background, shown about 1890. The Wyandotte Building was designed by the famous American architect, Daniel H. Burnham. (OHS)

TWO CHITTENDEN HOTELS have stood on this site at the northwest corner of Spring and High streets. This was the first, as it looked in 1891. The building was originally a business block, four stories high, but the owner, H. T. Chittenden, added two floors to the structure in 1890 and transformed it into a hotel that was regarded as one of the best in the city at the time. (OHS)

THEY DON'T MAKE RAILROAD STATIONS the way they used to, and the old Toledo & Ohio Station which looked like a cross between a Chinese pagoda and a Moroccan bathhouse, pretty well proves the point. The station was built in 1896, when, presumably, they should have known more restraint. (OHS)

HALLO, CENTRAL! The main exchange of the telephone company in 1896 had a lot of pretty young operators doing an Eyes Right! and an Eyes Left! for the photographer. The exchange in those days was on the third floor of a building at 26½ North High Street. (Bell)

ELECTRICITY was put to effective use almost immediately by enterprising merchants in the late nineteenth century--here is how the F. & R. Lazarus & Company Department Store looked by day and by night. (OHS)

THIS ELABORATELY GABLED BUILD-
ing was the headquarters of the Columbus
Fire Department on North Front Street
north of Gay Street at the turn of the century. It also housed Engine Company
No. 1. (OHS)

ONE OF THE HANDSOME HOMES in early Columbus was the residence of Francis
Sessions, a businessman who, with George
Tiviss as manager, established the city's
first telephone exchange. His house was on
the site of the modern Columbus Art Gal-
lery. (Bell)

NO NEW SCHOOL WAS COMPLETE without that architectural panache, a grand tower, during those years of expansion and building in the second half of the nineteenth century. Some of the examples of the school construction of that period are shown in these old pictures of the Fifth Avenue Public School *(above right)*, the High School (identification enough at the time) at Sixth Street and East Broad *(above left)*, the Twenty-Third Street School *(below)*, and the Franklinton School on the west side *(left)*. (CPL)

THIS STONE TOWER in Minerva Amusement Park used to be something of a mystery to Columbusites who gave it all sorts of romantic backgrounds, but it really was nothing more than a power booster station for the electric utility, built before the turn of the century. (C&SOE)

[ 61 ]

AN ELEGANT HOSTELRY in the growing-up days of Columbus was the renowned Park Hotel, seen here in its prime. It stood on High Street, at the corner of Goodale. (Weisheimer)

THE STREETCAR TRACKS were clogged with traffic on this day, probably in the 1890s, in front of the Franklin County Court House which stood in all its baroque splendor at the corner of Mound and High. (Weisheimer)

A MILITARY MOBILIZATION CENTER
called Cámp Bushnell, located on the east
side off East Broad Street at Drexel Avenue, was hastily organized at the outbreak
of the Spanish-American War in 1898.
Troops from all over the state arrived at
this railroad station *(left)*, to be transferred to the camp in buggies and wagons.
The ladies of the town were watching the
arriving soldiers *(below)* at the entrance
of the camp. (CD/CC-J)

PAGEANTRY AND PUFFERY were part of advertising of the Sells Brothers Circus that wintered in Columbus off Main Street, and called the city home. A rare photograph shows one of the circus wagons being drawn down a Columbus street by ten white horses sometime around 1900. (Weisheimer)

THE TELEPHONE was still very much a novelty and a mystery at the time the old Citizens Telephone Company of Columbus ran this advertisement in the *Ohio State Journal* before 1900. The company later was absorbed by Ohio Bell. (Weisheimer)

HELLO! PAPA WILL YOU BE HOME TO LUNCH?

WILLIAMS' BEST FLOUR

An exhibit of this Made-in-Columbus Flour will be shown at the Exposition,

JUNE 21 TO JULY 4

Bread, Cakes, Pies and Bakestuffs keep longer and stay fresh and crisp when they are baked with WILLIAMS' BEST FLOUR.

Baking is always a success when WILLIAMS' BEST FLOUR is used and you do not have to trust to luck.

WILLIAMS' BEST FLOUR is unbleached and guaranteed under the pure food act. If you will say WILLIAMS' BEST to the grocer when you are buying flour you can rest assured that you are buying absolutely the best flour at any price, and then, too, it's COLUMBUS MADE.

HARDESTY-
WILLIAMS
MILLING
COMPANY

COLUMBUS, OHIO.

COLUMBUS was a major milling center before 1900, and among the large flour companies headquartered in the capital was the Hardesty-Williams Milling Company, whose newspaper advertisment of a long-ago day is reproduced here. Among the company's several brands were Orange Blossom, Morning Glory, Monark, and Economy. (Weisheimer)

[ 63 ]

THE OLD TOD BARRACKS? Some experts say this is a photograph of the Tod Barracks which served Columbus during the Civil War. Others dispute the claim. The army barracks, at any rate, were on High Street near the old Union Station and not far from Goodale Street. There isn't any question that the building shown here, about 1900, was very, very old. (CD)

THIS COZY SCENE, photographed about the turn of the century, is believed to show prisoners in the Ohio Penitentiary Annex – trusties, no doubt – relaxing with good books, games, and guitar music. The stimulating effect of the tableau is further heightened by the dudish dress of the subjects. Was prison really that much fun in the good old days? (OHS)

PUBLIC SPEAKING was a highly regarded achievement at the turn of the century, and this group of earnest young men was studying the art of elocution at that time under the tutelage of Prof. Robert Fulton. Everyone stopped talking long enough for the photographer to take a picture. (CD)

THE STATUE of the German poet, Friedrich von Schiller, is the feature piece in the Columbus park named in his honor. The south side neighborhood, close to downtown, received hundreds of German immigrants during the nineteenth century and came to be known in later years as German Village. (OHS)

THE POOL at Indianola Park was one of the most popular summer fun spots in town. The bathhouse in the background was jammed the day this picture was taken early in the century, but the large pool is curiously entertaining only a handful of swimmers and bathers. (OHS)

[ 66 ]  LOOKING NORTH from the roof of the Great Southern Hotel at Main Street in 1901, this is the way High Street appeared to the people of the time. (CD)

THE TWENTIETH CENTURY was still very new when a photographer snapped this very clear picture of Broad and High, looking east on Broad Street. (CD)

OLENTANGY PARK

Looping-The-Loop
Olentangy Park, Columbu

OLD OLENTANGY PARK was a favorite of entertainment seekers who arrived on the north side of the city in streetcars of the High Street line *(above)*, to enjoy the rides of the amusement park. Death-defying acts were not unknown to the thrill-seekers of the early twentieth century, as the picture of an unruffled gentleman unconcerned about gravity *(right)* shows. The most popular ride, though, even if a little less wild, was the shoot-the-chutes *(below)*. (Weisheimer)

Shoot-The-Chutes, Olentangy Park, Columbus, Ohio.

[ 67 ]

AN IMPORTANT PART of Columbus life was the Masonic Temple on Fourth Street at Lynn Alley, shown here in a photograph taken about 1905. (Burke)

A FAMOUS CHURCH in old Columbus was the First Congregational Church at 70 East Broad Street. Its pastor, Washington Gladden, was equally famous in the community. The church, since razed, is shown as it looked about 1905. (Burke)

THE AIRSHIP *Knabenshue* thrilled people in Columbus and other Ohio cities when it flew overhead in the early years of the century. It is shown resting on the ground between flights over Toledo. (Burke)

*Storage Dam, Columbus, O.*

A DAM SITE BETTER than the story had it was Griggs Dam, shown here. Built as a storage dam in 1905 on the Olentangy River, Griggs Dam was the subject of the famous story, "The Day the Dam Broke," by humorist James Thurber. It never did break. Even if it had, according to the spoilsport experts, the water that burst loose never could have reached High Street, some miles away. (Burke)

THE HORSE-DRAWN VEHICLES of the old Central Union Telephone Company in Columbus line up for the photographer and posterity on a sunny autumn day in 1907. The main office of the company, in the background, stood at 33 North Third Street. (Bell)

ALICE ROOSEVELT *(left)*, daughter of Pres. Theodore Roosevelt, was among the honored guests at the ceremonies in 1906 unveiling the monument to martyred Pres. William McKinley, onetime governor of Ohio, at the High Street entrance to the State House. (OHS)

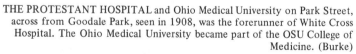

THE PROTESTANT HOSPITAL and Ohio Medical University on Park Street, across from Goodale Park, seen in 1908, was the forerunner of White Cross Hospital. The Ohio Medical University became part of the OSU College of Medicine. (Burke)

THE SECOND BUILDING of
the *Columbus Dispatch* at
Gay and High streets was destroyed by fire on April 9,
1907. This is the way the gut-
ted building looked in the cold
light of day, after firemen
had put out the blaze. (CD)

THE THIRD BUILDING
occupied by the *Colum-
bus Dispatch* during its
long history of publication
was this handsome struc-
ture at Gay and High. It
served the newspaper from
1907 until November 22,
1925. (CD)

[ 71 ]

A RAKISH GROUP of students from the Starling Ohio Medical College, later to become the Ohio State University College of Medicine, came together for this group portrait in 1908. Two of them, it will be noted, were women. (CD)

THE OLD CENTRAL MARKET at the corner of Rich Street and South Fourth as it looked prior to World War I. Off to the left, directly under the sign "Outfit—Cash or Credit" is another advertisement on the wall of the building in the background for "The Market Exchange Saloon and Restaurant, Fred Haynes, Prop." (OHS)

SAINT FRANCIS HOSPITAL at 311 East State Street near the Columbus Public Library celebrated its one hundredth year of service in 1950. The building, erected in 1849 for the Starling Medical College, represented a formidable architectural achievement for its day in a community that was only 37 years removed from its virgin-forest beginnings. An order of nuns, the Franciscan Sisters of the Poor, run the hospital. (OHS)

ONCE A FAMILIAR SIGHT on Columbus streets were wagons like this of the Troy Laundry in 1908. The fancy fringe affair draped over the horse was pretty effective in shooing away the flies. The driver had to fend for himself. (Burke)

THE CHAMPIONS FROM COLUMBUS in the American Association posed on a *Columbus Dispatch* postcard in 1906. The team won the league title twice. (Weisheimer)

HOBBLE SKIRTS made life difficult for ladies boarding streetcars, or getting off, back in the pre-World War I days when this trolley ran on Columbus streets. The customers never had to complain about a lack of air, though. (CGS)

A GAS COMPANY repair crew starts out to work on a street job, pushcart, pipes, spare bricks, and all, in the early years of the century. (CGS

A DAZZLING MODERN KITCHEN for its day, sometime around the turn of the century, was this domestic work center in a palatial Columbus home. The coal stove, the centerpiece of the room, provided heat and was used for cooking and baking, and heated the water in the enormous water tank to the right. Notice the hods of coal at the right. The sink with its hot and cold running water was no mean feature for the time, either. (CGS)

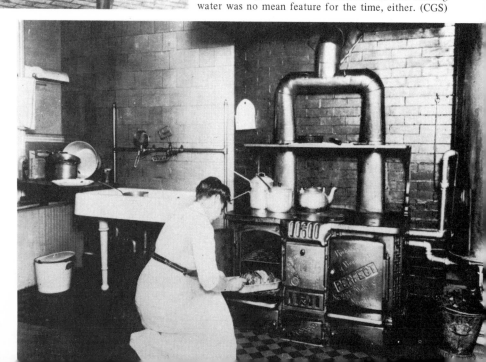

NEDDERMEYER'S BAND stopped its tootling and oom-pah-pahing long enough one fine day in 1910 to pose in front of a bandstand in the park, but the precise location is not known. As the lettering on the drum suggests, Columbus in those days was known as the Arch City because of the arches over High Street, used for nighttime electrical illumination. (CD)

COBBLESTONED HIGH STREET, at the intersection of Long Street, was a jumble of buildings and advertising signs when this picture was taken in 1910. And here is a close-up of the famous overhead arch which was used for street lighting in those days. (CD)

LONG & HIGH 1910

THE SOUTHERN THEATER on Main Street near High showed "Shubert Attractions" at the time, probably around 1910. The feature presentation that day was *The House of Bondage*. Notice the spiffy Baker Electric automobile parked along the curb. (CD)

THE COLONIAL THEATER, one of the city's earliest movie houses, was in its prime when it was showing "De Luxe Photo-Plays" at reasonable prices: Downstairs seating cost 10 cents for adults, 5 cents for children. It was five cents for everybody in the balcony. The street-level store, by the way, sold Oliver typewriters. (OHS)

THE OLD HIGH STREET THEATER was in this building next door to the Chittenden Hotel. Buckingham's Academy of Dancing was upstairs, at 219½ High Street. (OHS)

DETROIT WASN'T THE ONLY CITY that manufactured automobiles as the country scrambled to get on wheels early in the present century. An advertisement in the February 19, 1910, issue of the old *Literary Digest* touted the famous Columbus Electric, the Columbus Buggy Company's answer to the automobile age. At the bottom of the ad, the company stated that it also turned out gasoline-powered cars under the name of Firestone-Columbus. (CPL)

LIKE MINUTEMEN on motorcycles, these service men of the telephone company stand ready to roar into action in 1910. The Central Union Telephone Building at Third Street and Lynn Alley still stands in 1977. The service men were, from left to right, W. O. Stricklin, E. C. Groce, C. H. Milborne, C. Edwards, L. E. Mowbray, J. S. Strayer, and W. L. Davis. (Bell)

LOOKING more like a country chateau than a commercial city hotel is the old Hotel Vendome, in its day one of the more elegant places to stop in Columbus. It was built in 1912 and stood on South Third Street, opposite the capitol. (OHS)

LONG DRESSES and flowery, plumed hats were the style among women; straw hats and peg-top trousers led men's styles back about 1910. The stylish corner in this photo is the intersection of Gay Street and High, looking east on Gay. The open-air streetcar made public transportation fun. The corner building on the left is the *Columbus Dispatch*. The building on the right-hand side of the intersection sports "The Gay Academy," but gay was an innocent word in those days. (Burke)

Gay Street looking East from High Street, Columbus, Ohio.

NOTHING SEEMED TO LAST LONG in the old days. This is a view from Third Street showing the razing in 1910 of the First Presbyterian Church that stood at the corner of State and Third. It was torn down to make way for the Hartman Building. Notice the top of the capitol showing above the shell of the doomed structure. (Burke)

THE WATERFRONT between State and Rich streets about 1910. (CC-J)

WHEN COLUMBUS CELEBRATED its centennial in 1912, elaborate preparations for the attendant festivities were made. A speaker's platform and reviewing stand were erected on High Street in front of the capitol *(above)*, bunting was strung everywhere as on this downtown intersection *(below)* where open-air streetcars, horse-drawn buggies, new-fangled automobiles, and daredevil pedestrians competed for space. When the parade came, floats such as one advertising a dairy and carrying a milkmaid and a genuine cow *(opposite page, top)*, were the main attractions. And the state government was no laggard either, as the bunting-decorated State House *(opposite page, bottom)* indicates. (CD)

FLOOD Col's. O. Mar. 25-1913
RESCUE STATION

WHEN A TERRIBLE FLOOD hit in March 1913, destruction was everywhere, bridges collapsed, houses were swept away, and general misery was the result. The flood had just about reached its peak when refugees were brought by rowboat to the hastily set up rescue station at Rich and Center streets *(above)*. Not only people suffered terribly, even the animals were affected. This poor horse *(left)* was trapped in the floating debris and carried away by the waters, coming to a rest near State and Mill streets. And when the waters had receded, people were standing around in a daze, unable to fathom yet that their homes and businesses were in ruins. The photograph below shows families on the west side inspecting the damage. The fury of the flood can be seen in the tilted houses and the big streetcar, tossed on its side like a toy, far from its tracks. (CPL/OHS/Burke)

**THE WORLD'S FIRST FILLING STATION** was this one in Columbus, built in 1913. It was at the corner of Oak and Young streets. The Standard Oil Company went on from here to more elaborate stations, but the drive-through design of this first one still makes it a standout. (CC-J)

**TRAFFIC CONTROL** was achieved in a much simpler way around 1914 as this Columbus street scene of that time demonstrates. Traffic policemen regulated the flow of vehicles and pedestrians, and some, as in this instance, were protected from the overhead sun by an umbrella smartly lettered with "Stop" and "Go" instructions. (OHS)

THERE WASN'T MUCH TRAFFIC on North High Street about 1914, but the double-deck streetcar headed towards downtown was an eyestopper as it paused for passengers in front of the busy Union Station Arcade. (OHS)

FRANK NIXON

PRESIDENT NIXON'S FATHER? Nobody knows for sure, but this old photograph of a Columbus streetcar and its motorman, identified as one Frank Nixon, possibly could star Pres. Richard M. Nixon's father, who also was named Frank and who also worked for a time as a motorman for the Columbus street railway. The story is that he froze his ears operating a car with an open cab and decided to head for the sunny clime of Southern California. (OHS)

THE STREET RAILROAD in Columbus scored a sensational breakthrough in 1914 with the introduction of this fantastic double-deck vehicle. It ran for a while on the High Street line but proved to be impractical. (C&SOE)

[ 84 ]

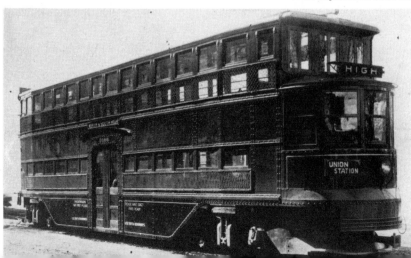

BROAD AND HIGH is generally acknowledged to be the busiest intersection in Columbus at any time, but during this period in 1915 it must have set new high marks for activity. Opposing forces are shown at work here. In the background, center, the Old Deshler Block is being demolished to make way for the new Deshler Hotel. At the same time, the street railway company is laying new car tracks in the center of the street, and it appears that all the street pavement has been torn up. (Burke)

THE LAZARUS DEPARTMENT STORE had its own electric power plant, built in 1895. The generating facility was razed in 1925 to make way for a store expansion project. The power plant shown was at West Town Street and South Wall. (Burke)

SEVEN MEN, A BOY, AND A DOG posed for the photographer one day in 1915. The men were service employees of the old Ohio State Telephone Company, from left to right, W. M. Martin, A. R. Lindsey, A. Miller, O. C. Clemens, J. Williams, R. Sprouse, and J. Green. The boy is unidentified, but the dog's name is Teddy. (Bell)

RACING BLOODS found their pleasure out at the old Driving Park, where automobiles roared around the dirt track at unbelievable speeds. The action here took place about 1915. Eddie Rickenbacker must have raced this course many times during his successful career as a race driver before going on to fame as an aviator. (OHS)

WORLD WAR I came, and a major contribution by Columbus to the American war effort was Elsie Janis, a native daughter (real name, Elsie Bierbower), who became world-famous as "The Sweetheart of the A.E.F." Miss Janis, a comedienne-singer on the vaudeville stage, also was a talented musical-comedy librettist and composer. In 1917 and 1918, she entertained troops of the American Expeditionary Force in France in the front lines and gained national popularity. The picture shows her as she looked as the star of a full-length motion picture, *Women in War,* in 1940. (CC-J)

A WARTIME VERSION of an old peacetime game was played on the State House lawn during the first World War in Columbus. People making contributions to the war chest were allowed to throw a ball at heads stuck through portholes representing the German crown prince, the Kaiser, and Field Marshall von Hindenburg. Accurate head shots rang the bell, even if they did not know how to spell the enemy field marshall's name. (CD)

[ 87 ]

AMONG THE MANY contributions of Ohio State University to the Allied effort in World War I was this airplane laboratory testing aeronautical theories and airplane construction. (Copyright by Ohio State University Press)

CLASPED HANDS and all the other general signs of discomfiture marked this formal photograph of the Board of Control and staff of Ohio State's humor publication, the *Sun Dial*, in 1917. The two young gentlemen flanking the bottom row (seated) were destined to become famous far beyond the limits of the Ohio State campus: Elliott Nugent, far left, as an actor-producer in New York and Hollywood: James Thurber, far right, as a foremost American humor writer and artist. Seated between them, left to right, are Leon Friedman, Prof. Joseph S. Myers, George Packer, Prof. William L. (Billy) Graves, and Herman Achauer. In the second row are, left to right, Maurice Mullay, Ralph McCombs, Ruth Young, Eleanor Lewis, Elsie McGee, Margaret Teachnor, Carlene Hermann, Carson Blair, and Paul Crider. In the top row, left to right, are Newton Thatcher, Jack Pierce, and Stanley Koch. (OSU)

EDDIE RICKENBACKER was Columbus' home-grown war hero. Before the war, he already had become well-known as an automobile race driver *(above),* but his major claim to fame was his career as a pilot in the 94th Pursuit Squadron of the U.S. Air Service, the leading American flying group in World War I. They fought in rickety planes against the famous "German Flying Circus" commanded by Manfred von Richthofen, better known as the "Red Baron," and Rickenbacker scored 27 kills, making him the leading air ace of the American forces. He is seen at right, far from the Scioto and Olentangy rivers, leaning against his slender fighter plane on an airfield near Toul, France, on May 5, 1918. His birthplace at 1334 Livingstone Avenue *(below)* was photographed in 1943.

(CC-J/CPD/CC-J)

THE END OF WORLD WAR I brought thousands of people into the downtown streets of Columbus to parade and whoop it up for the armistice agreement. The wartime memorial arch is in the background. The date was November 11, 1918. (CD)

THE HERO BACK HOME! Eddie Rickenbacker, America's leading air ace in World War I, posed with his mother, Mrs. William Rickenbacker, and his sister, Emma, on his return to Columbus after the war. (CPD)

AS IT LOOKED, COMING AND GOING, the automobile named after the most famous Columbus son to come out of World War I, Eddie Rickenbacker. The design of the Rickenbacker borrowed heavily from the aeronautical field, appropriately enough. Notice the streamlined headlights and the fuselage effect in the rear, The Rickenbacker was manufactured for two years after the war before it was shot down by its competitors. (CC-J)

[ 91 ]

A PANORAMIC VIEW of an outdoor graduation ceremony on the famed oval of the Ohio State University campus in June 1919: University Hall rears high in the background. (OSU)

LOOKING LIKE a holdover from the medieval past, this jumble
of towers and turrets was the beloved armory on the Ohio State
University Oval, not far from the Fifteenth Street entrance. It was
built in 1899. The view dates back to sometime around 1920. (Burke)

CHARLES (CHIC) HARLEY, who reached his peak as a football
star at Ohio State University immediately after World War I, still is
rated the best gridder who ever played for the Bucks; a high dis-
tinction at a university known for its outstanding football teams.
He was OSU's first all-American. (Burke)

POLICE CHIEF HARRY FRENCH (center of photo, with white
hair) was the central figure when the cornerstone was laid for the
new Central Police Station destined to be part of the new Civic
Center at Broad Street and Marconi Boulevard. (CD)

THE OLD CITY HALL on East State Street was all but destroyed by a fire on the night of January 12, 1921. This was the way it looked the next day, a burned-out shell. (CD)

THE CORNER OF BROAD & THIRD, around which so much of modern Columbus is built, was just a hole in the ground back in 1920. Excavation was underway for the Rowland Building. (CD)

COLUMBUS AUDITORIUM, at Town and Front streets, was the center of civic life in the early 1920s. Traffic lights and No-Parking signs still were rarities in those days. The old auditorium, too small to meet later demands, eventually was sold to the Lazarus Department Store and converted into a store annex. (CD)

[ 94 ]

NORTH HIGH STREET in front of the capitol back at the beginning of the 1920s. (Bell)

THE OHIO STATE CAMPUS looking north in 1922! To the upper left is the skeleton of the new Ohio Stadium, then under construction. (OSU)

OHIO STADIUM nearing completion: despite its enormous size and its initial seating capacity of 63,000, the stadium was completed within thirteen months after the first shovel of dirt was turned. It was dedicated on October 21, 1922. (OSU)

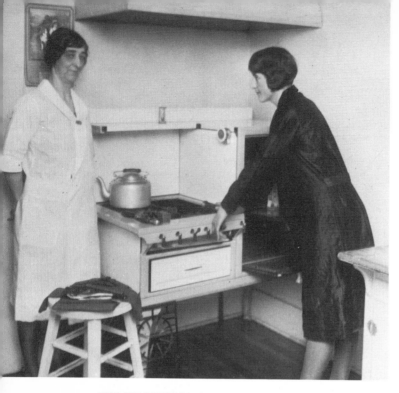

THE MODERN ERA in home
cooking had begun when a home
service expert of the Columbus
Gas & Fuel Company showed a
housewife how to use her slick
new gas range, the latest word in
kitchen efficiency at the time--
probably in the early 1920s. (CGS)

THE TIN LIZZIES had taken over the streets by 1924, as this picture looking west on Broad Street
from Third shows, but some of the horse-and-buggy diehards were still fighting for parking space. (OHS)

THE CITADEL of the American Insurance Union, the first real skyscraper in Columbus, climbs into the sky sometime in 1926. Said to have been the fifth tallest building in the world at the time of its construction, it was better known as the A.I.U. Tower; later, as the LeVeque-Lincoln Tower when it had passed into the hands of Leslie L. LeVeque and John Lincoln in April 1945. The great building at the corner of Broad and Front streets was dedicated on September 21, 1927. It is 55 stories high and 555.5 feet in height. Ground was broken in September 1924, for the building designed by architect C. Howard Crane of Detroit, and the estimated cost of the project was $8 million. (LeVeque Enterprises)

THE JACK DEMPSEY-Gene Tunney heavyweight championship fight on the night of September 23, 1926, aroused great interest in Columbus. A huge crowd gathered in front of the Columbus Dispatch Building and listened to the blow-by-blow description of the fight on radio, relayed to them by loudspeakers. The State House is in the background. (CD)

[ 97 ]

IT WAS THE END of a theatrical era when the key was turned, locking the doors of the old B. F. Keith Theater on East Gay Street for the last time on March 26, 1926. (CD)

WARNER BAXTER, a native son, made Columbus proud through his successful acting career in Hollywood over a period of some thirty years. Baxter, a matinee idol who became the second actor to win the Academy Award, began his career in the silent pictures of the late 1920s. He died in Hollywood at age 58 in 1951. (CC-J)

THE OLENTANGY RIVER overflowed its banks in 1927, flooding the lowland athletic fields of Ohio State University. The waters lapped at the gates of Ohio Stadium and trapped a car whose driver put his passenger on the hood as "pilot." (OSU)

PORT COLUMBUS, the new landing field for the city, was dedicated on Monday, July 4, 1929. All three planes in view are tri-motor types belonging to Transcontinental Air Transport (TAT), the forerunner of today's TWA. (OHS)

THE AIR AGE was still young on July 8, 1929, when coast-to-coast passenger service utilizing trains by night and planes by day had its beginning. The crack Pennsylvania Railroad train, "The Airway Limited ," is departing from the station at Port Columbus, the eastern terminal for Transcontinental Air Transport (TAT Air Line) and a key transfer point in the unique system. It took three days to cross the nation by this dual-transportation method, but that was the fastest way there was. (CC-J)

THE COLUMBUS WATERFRONT and the old skyline, undistinguished except for the A.I.U. Citadel (left), seen from the west bank of the Scioto River on June 6, 1929. (Weisheimer)

PERHAPS THE MOST SENSATIONAL murder trial in the history of Columbus was the one in which an Ohio State University faculty member, Dr. James H. Snook, was tried for the murder of a coed named Theora Hix. The trial took place in the summer of 1929 and Dr. Snook was found guilty. He was executed in the Ohio State Penitentiary's electric chair. Dr. Snook is shown here (seated) as he was arraigned on the murder charge. In the photograph are, left to right, Sheriff Harry Paul of Franklin County, Dr. Snook, John Seidel and E. O. Ricketts, attorneys for the defense, and prosecutor John J. Chester, Jr. (CPD)

THE FLOOD CONTROL PROGRAM was well under way in 1929 when this steamshovel was scooping up earth along the east bank of the Scioto River, close to the Main Street Bridge, preparing the way for the new retaining wall. (Weisheimer)

# Making Ready for the Future: 1920 to 1950

COLUMBUS, upon reaching the 1920s, hesitated on the threshold of the future so clearly visible on the far horizon. Its people were obviously reluctant to part with the pleasant environment they had created over the first century of the city's existence. By instinct, by design, and by accident, they had achieved the kind of admirable ambience that most other cities strive for, but seldom achieve. The capital, in the postwar years, found itself enjoying a nice balance between urbanity and the solid farm philosophy that was so pervasive in the agricultural countryside of Central Ohio which made an island of the city. The smoke from thousands of chimneys was not strong enough yet to cancel out entirely the sweet smell of newly mown hay.

People in Columbus liked to refer to their hometown as the biggest small city in the country, and perhaps it was. The capital had chosen its own pace—tranquility over turmoil. But there was destiny to reckon with. It had the strength to take the city beyond itself.

The terrible flood of 1913 was an example. As devastating as that disaster was, it brought about a lot of lasting good. The lowland areas of the city's west side had been inundated so many times since the founding of Franklinton that the inhabitants had come to look upon the msifortune as an inevitable visitation. There had been about a dozen floods in some seventy-five years, but it took the 1913 disaster with its terrible property damage and loss of life to galvanize the city into permanent corrective action.

The flood control program also resulted in a cleanup of the shabby shores of the Scioto that seemed, in turn, to spark an even larger civic beautification program. Trouble often can be turned to such advantage. When a raging fire consumed the stately City Hall on East State Street on the night of January 12, 1921, it led to the construction of a new city administration headquarters building down near the riverfront, west of Front Street, in an area that had been filled with sagging, disreputable old structures.

The new City Hall on Marconi Boulevard, just north of Broad Street, was finished in 1926. In a second stage of construction, an East Wing was added to the building in 1934. Meanwhile, a modern Central Police Station was built nearby, also on Marconi Boulevard. It was opened in 1929.

The blossoming civic center on the riverfront was a natural site for the new Federal Building and U. S. Court House. Its addition in 1933 added new class to the entire downtown area as did a nearby State project. Close by, on Front Street south of Broad, the new State Office Building was built at a cost of close to six million dollars. Most remarkable of all, the city's first real skyscraper soared high into the clouds at the northeast corner of Broad and Front. It was the American Insurance Union (A.I.U.) Citadel, whose 55-story height of 555½ feet made it one of the tallest buildings in the world at the time.

The skyscraper was finished just before the nation and the city lapsed into a state of deep depression, followed by an all-engrossing fight for survival in World War II. It was a fifteen-year period of marking time and maintaining the status quo. Once again, as it had in past wars, Columbus served as a vital mobilization center with its Fort Hayes, headquarters of the Fifth Army Corps.

Another portent of future developments came about in the World War II defense effort. Columbus was chosen to be the site of an enormous airplane manufacturing industry, the plant of the Curtiss-Wright Corporation. There always had been a certain industrial element in the Columbus economy, but this development represented a breakthrough. One large industry often has a way of attracting other manufacturing establishments, and so it was in Columbus in the immediate postwar years, as General Motors and other large companies elected to build new plants on the periphery of the Ohio State Capital.

The addition of industry to the foundation base of government, commerce, science, and education added tremendous new strength to Columbus. Growth and greatness were made inevitable. It was just a matter of time. But no matter how brightly the future beckoned, the people who knew the city best still paused on the threshhold of tomorrow to look back, with genuine affection, on yesterday's Columbus. It will not be forgotten.

[ 102 ]

WHILE TODAY'S MOTORISTS may yearn for "the good old days," this view of Town and Third Avenue in 1930 suggests that parking probably was more of a problem than it is today. There certainly isn't much space for moving traffic, thanks to the angle parking of those days. (CD)

THE TROUBLE-BESET OHIO PENITENTIARY was struck by a tornado in 1929. The twister did severe damage to the institution as the photograph shows. Several convicts died in the collapsing walls and flying bricks. One of the bodies is shown on a stretcher in the foreground while two trusties look over the rubble in amazement. (CPD)

THEN, ON APRIL 22, 1930, a fire broke out in the west wing of the penitentiary which raged throughout the night, killing 319 prisoners and injuring 231—the worst prison disaster in American history. (CPD)

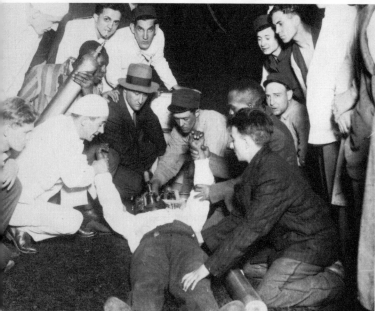

THE OHIO STATE PENITENTIARY
fire left many prisoners without a roof
over their heads, and tents had to be
erected for temporary housing on the
baseball grounds behind the power
house *(above)*. The holocaust ulti-
mately claimed a total of 319 lives in
spite of valiant efforts of prisoners,
physicians, and prison officials to help
those who had been injured. An uncon-
scious convict is being given first aid
*(left)*. All the while, soldiers of the
Ohio National Guard *(below)* took up
precautionary positions outside the
penitentiary to guard against potential
trouble. (CPD/Perry Cragg/CPD)

PROGRESS IN POLICE WORK is evident in this proudly-posed picture of Columbus police officials with their department's sensational new "radio cruiser" in 1932. (CC-J)

EVERY NOW AND THEN, out of the learned faculty ranks in every university, there emerges the rare individual who wins the hearts of his students as well as their minds. Ohio State has had more than its fair share of such remarkable men and women in its teaching lists; too many to give credit to all of them, but a representative sample would include the three long-time faculty members shown here: Prof. William (Billy) Graves *(right)* beloved teacher of English; Dr. John Wilce *(below left)* an outstanding teacher and a nationally-renowned football coach who moved the Ohio State Buckeyes into the big-time ranks during his tenure as coach, 1913-1928, and Dr. Henry Spencer *(below right)* a gentle man of great erudition who made generations of Ohio Staters love political science almost as much as they loved their professor. (OSU)

[ 105 ]

A NEW WAY TO GO was the latest in urban transportation, a trackless trolley, also known as a trolley coach, seen in 1933 at Broad and High. (C&SOE)

A MILESTONE in the improvement of the Columbus waterfront was the construction of the new Central High School on the west bank of the Scioto River, facing downtown. This photograph shows the ceremonial program dedicating the new school on April 2, 1932. (CD)

WORKMEN of the George J. Igel Company hoist a new 80-foot electrical pole into place at an outlying intersection made even more strategic--for the workmen, anyway--by the Corner Grill. It was October 1933, and Prohibition had just been repealed. The happy event is reflected in the store sign advertising beer for 5 cents! Notice also the tall gasoline pumps out front, at the curb. Gasoline and drink did mix in those days. (C&SOE)

THE DEPRESSION WAS JUST SETTLING on the city and the nation when this picture of West Goodale Street, looking west from the corner of Pennsylvania Avenue, was snapped. The area shown was part of the district known as Flytown, which was among the hardest hit by the depression. (Weisheimer)

URBAN RENEWAL at the Columbus waterfront scored a triumph when the newly completed Federal Building in the downtown area just north of Broad Street was dedicated in 1934. The recently constructed Central Police Station can be seen partially in the lower right corner. (Burke)

THE I.O.O.F. TEMPLE at 198 South High Street was an old downtown Columbus landmark from the nineteenth century until a devastating fire destroyed it in February 1936. The most tragic aspect of the fire was that five firemen died battling the blaze. (CD)

ALL OHIO WAS SHOCKED when the grand new State Office Building at 65 South Front Street on the Scioto River, just south of Broad Street, was ripped by an explosion of escaping gas. About $1,000,000 damage was caused to the $6,500,000 building. Seven men were killed and about forty were injured by the blast that tore away part of the facade on the river side of the thirteen-story structure. Shown in pictures taken after the explosion are a view of the damaged side of the building from the Scioto River *(below)*, and a close-up of the most severely affected area *(right)*. (CC-J)

COACH FRANCIS SCHMIDT, famed as the originator and master of the "razzle-dazzle" style of football, leans anxiously towards the playing field in a tense moment during an Ohio State game sometime in the early 1930s. Schmidt was coach of Ohio State's Buckeyes from 1934 to 1940. (OSU)

HE WENT UP TO SEE HER ONE TIME! Mae West, looking like Little Bo Peep, greets a somewhat sheepish reporter for the *Ohio State Journal*, Ben Hayes, in her Hotel Deshler-Wallick suite. The time was 1936. Miss West was in town for a week-long appearance on the stage of the Palace Theater. Hayes, christened Bernard, was at the beginning of a distinguished career in journalism that took him, eventually, to the staff of the *Citizen-Journal* and a daily column. (CC-J)

JOURNALIST AT WORK: Johnny Jones actually was more of a Columbus institution than a journalist, although he was that, serving as a columnist for the *Columbus Dispatch* for many years. He first came to the attention of Columbus as a frenetic cheerleader at OSU. After graduation, he stayed in the public eye as manager of the Majestic Theater, and then the Southern Theater, before settling down to the more sedentary life of a newspaper columnist. He almost always wore spats, a heavy raccoon coat (in winter), a scarf, and a derby hat. The pipe was also a standard fixture. (CC-J)

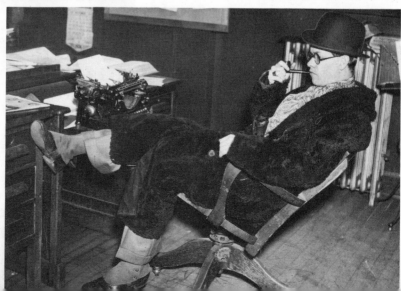

AN ARMY of spruced-up service representatives of Columbus
Gas Company, men and women alike, pose for the photographer before starting out on their rounds. The time is in the
middle thirties. (CGS)

A SELF-CONSCIOUS LOCAL HERO, James Thurber, the
famous humorist and artist, visited Columbus in November
1938 for a world-premiere showing of the motion picture
*The Male Animal,* based on his story whose setting was the
Ohio State University campus. Thurber is shown here in his
Deshler-Wallick Hotel suite with his wife. (CC-J)

ANNA MARIE HAHN, convicted of the murder of a 78-year-old Cincinnati man, was the first woman
to die in the electric chair of the Ohio Penitentiary. She was found guilty after a long, sensational
trial in the autumn of 1937, sentenced to death on November 6, 1937, and electrocuted on December 7, 1938. In a posthumous letter, she admitted poisoning four elderly men. The case attracted widespread national attention and press coverage. Reporters milled about in the lobby of the penitentiary
covering the execution story *(below right).* The newsman in the center with the fedora and cigar is
James Kilgallen, star correspondent of the International News Service and father of the late columnist
Dorothy Kilgallen. (CPD/Press Club of Columbus)

WHEN CELEBRITIES MEET, sometimes they kiss. Air hero Eddie Rickenbacker met film star Peggy Ann Garner in the office of Ohio governor Frank J. Lausche one day in August 1945, and they came together in a grand osculation. The governor hovers over his pair of visitors solicitously. (CC-J)

THE GREAT SPRAWL of buildings and facilities constituting Fort Hayes in Columbus, as it looked in 1944, is best appreciated in this aerial view. The Defense Department abandoned the historic installation some three years later. (CD)

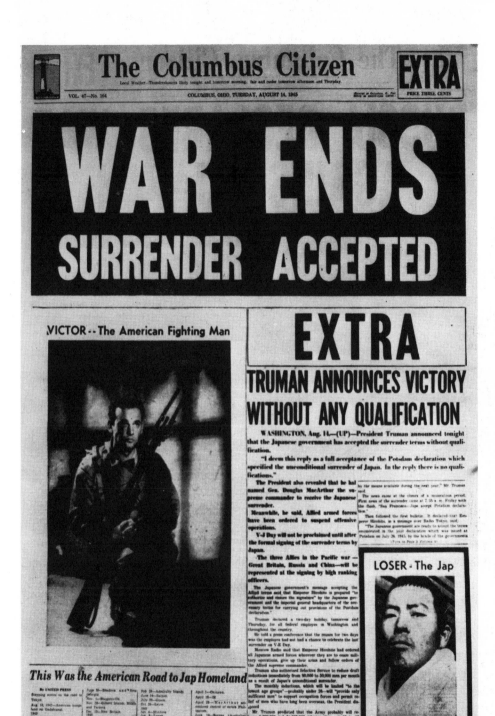

WHEN JAPAN SURRENDERED, ending World War II, the *Columbus Citizen* bannered the news on that historic date, August 14, 1945. The afternoon Scripps-Howard daily later merged with the *Ohio State Journal,* a morning newspaper. (CC-J)

THE BOY AND THE GENERAL: Curtis LeMay was a serious-looking young man about to graduate from South High School in Columbus when the portrait at right was taken. Less than twenty years later, as a four-star general, head of the United States Air Force's Strategic Air Command, and a war hero, Curtis LeMay and his wife watched the Ohio-Illinois football game in Ohio Stadium on November 19, 1945. (CC-J)

THE FLAG COMES DOWN for the last time at old Fort Hayes on this day in 1947 *(below)*. The great military installation dated back to the early 1860s when it had served as a Civil War arsenal, then as a military post, and finally as the headquarters of the Fifth Corps Area of the United States Army. It was called Columbus barracks until 1923, when it was renamed in honor of Pres. Rutherford B. Hayes, a former Ohio governor. The farewell address *(left)* was given by Gen. Robert S. Beightler, who had commanded Ohio's 37th Division in the Pacific Theater during World War II. Seated on his right is Ohio governor Thomas Herbert, wearing two-tone shoes. (CD)

O'SHAUGHNESSY DAM, named after water commissioner Jerry O'Shaughnessy, as it looked on July 12, 1945, when the waters of the Scioto River were going over the three-foot flashboards, marking the highest July stage for the river in many years. (CC-J)

LIGHTNING STRUCK the Broad Street Bridge over the Scioto River during a thunderstorm on August 21, 1947, causing considerable damage to the structure. (CD)

THE CALM BEFORE THE STORM: A sharply-etched aerial view shows the Ohio State University slumbering in the bright summer sunlight one day early in the 1940s—just before the postwar explosion of student enrollment and campus expansion that added scores of new buildings to the site. And milk shakes at Hennick's on North High Street near the Fifteenth Avenue main entrance to the campus were part of the scene for these bobby-soxers and their pipe-smoking friend in 1947 *(left)* as much as the huge skeleton of a mastodon *(below)* in Orton Hall, that was recovered from a field not far from Columbus. (OSU/CD)

*Facing page:* PERHAPS THE MOST FAMOUS PLACE on the OSU campus is this idyllic spot, a corner of the fabled Mirror Lake whose sulphurous waters smelled like perfume to generations of love-smitten students. (OSU)

[ 116 ]

HERE IS LIVING PROOF why Ohio State and Columbus are known as the capital of collegiate football—Saturday sell-out crowds as this one on November 20, 1948, are a common sight at Ohio Stadium. (Bell)

[ 118 ]

THIS WAS THE CENTRAL DISTRICT of Columbus in 1949, just before the building boom of the post-war era began. Dowtown is east of the bend in the Scioto River, easily discernible in this panoramic view. (CD)

MANY MAGNIFICENT MANSIONS lined East Broad Street at one time. Most of them disappeared under the pressure of progress, but some, like the one at 580 East Broad *(above)* survived. It was built in 1886 by Clinton D. Firestone, president of Columbus Buggy Company. The mansion was sold in 1914 to Columbus Mutual Insurance Company which occupied it for twenty-eight years. Later it became the home office of the Midland Mutual Life Insurance Company. (CD)

AMONG THE MEN who came to prominence in the postwar years in Columbus was this fist-pounding attorney, James W. Shocknessy, who guided the destinies of the Ohio Turnpike Commission as chairmain since its organization in 1949. (Ohio Turnpike Commission)

EVEN HIS POLITICAL ENEMIES acknowledged that the city administrations of thrice-elected mayor, James A. Rhodes (right), during the period from 1944 to January 12, 1953, represented a period of dynamic development for Columbus. Rhodes, who went on to become state auditor and governor, is shown here with another political luminary in the capital city, United States Senator John W. Bricker, former governor and vice-presidential running mate of Thomas E. Dewey in the 1944 Presidential campaign. (Cleveland News)

STATION WBNS-TV was just building its studio off the Olentangy River Road, near the end of Spring Street, in the spring of 1949. The transmitting tower in the background had already been completed, and shortly thereafter the station began telecasting on Channel 10. The Control Room of the station is at left. (WBNS-TV)

WHEN TELEVISION WAS NEW in Columbus in 1950, a young, aspiring comic named Jonathan Winters came to the capital city from his native Dayton in search of success. His talent was spotted by Station WBNS-TV and he was given the starring emcee-comic roles on two shows. He is shown at right on the set of a program called "Winter Wonderland." Above, he exchanges quips with another performer in the "Gamboree" program cast. Gambrinus Beer was the sponsor. (WNBS-TV)

A NIGHTTIME SCENE at the busiest corner of Columbus, Broad and High, in the late hours of a summer night in the early 1950s. The lights on the marquee of the famous Deshler Hilton Hotel blinked out a decade later. (CC-J)

[ 122 ]

SNOW COVERED THE STATE HOUSE on this blizzardy day in February 1950. (CC-J)

OLD POLITICAL FOES were brought together in Columbus during the 1952 Presidential campaign when Ohio's senior U.S. senator, Robert A. Taft, joined General Eisenhower in campaigning for votes in Ohio. They are in this open touring car on a nice summer day, Taft to the left and Ike to the right, as it drives up to the steps of the State House. Broad Street is in the background. (Burke)

STILL IN USE as a dwelling in the 1950s is this old house on South Gift Street which once served as the city's first post office in the Franklinton section. (CC-J)

MRS. MARY AGNES THURBER, mother of the famous American humorist, James Thurber, visited with a friend, Mrs. Millicent Easter, and Mrs. Mildred Fisher, the sister-in-law of Mrs. Thurber, in her suite at the Southern Hotel shortly after her eighty-sixth birthday in May 1952. (CC-J)

SOME OF THE BEST baseball ever played outside the major leagues was seen by Columbus fans in old Red Bird Stadium *(above)*, acknowledged to be one of the best facilities of its kind in the country. The Columbus Red Birds of the American Association were for a long time the leading farm club of the St. Louis Cardinals of the National League. At left is the entrance to Red Bird Stadium on West Mound Street on a cold March day, just before the 1951 season opened. (CC-J)

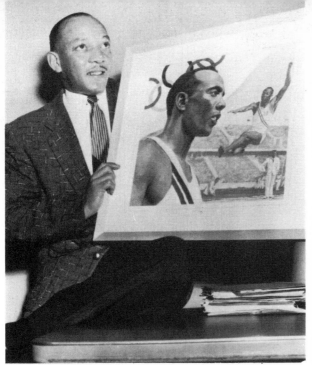

THE GREATEST TRACK ATHLETE of his day, and the greatest track star of the first fifty years of the century in the results of an Associated Press poll, was Jesse Owens of Ohio State. His record-breaking performances in Ohio Stadium and on the fields of Olympic competition in 1936 gave him fame beyond that ever achieved by a track star before him. He is seen above, in 1954, holding up a painting of himself inspired by his sensational wins in the 1936 Olympic Games. (Cleveland News)

A LIVING LEGEND on the Ohio State University campus in 1952 was Bill North. North, then 79, was the watchman at Ohio Stadium, a job which the university had given him in 1943 after he had reached compulsory retirement age of 70 and had to turn in his badge as campus cop. He had been hired as the first OSU policeman in 1908, staying on to become perhaps the best-loved personality on campus. (CC-J)

[ 125 ]

WOODY HAYES, Ohio State's most famous football coach, began his phenomenal career with the Buckeyes in 1951. Soon he would be pacing the sidelines, worrying about the events on the field. Some things never change. (OSU)

# Index

[ 128 ]